Devolution in the United Kingdom

Russell Deacon and Alan Sandry

Edinburgh University Press

This book is dedicated to Mandy Deacon, Garry Deacon, Tracey Deacon, Vivienne James and Wally Barnes. My kind and loving family.
Dr Russell Deacon

© Russell Deacon and Alan Sandry, 2007

Edinburgh University Press Ltd
22 George Square, Edinburgh

Typeset in 11/13pt Monotype Baskerville by
Servis Filmsetting Ltd, Manchester, and
printed and bound in Spain by
GraphyCems

A CIP record for this book is available from the British Library

ISBN 978 0 7486 2416 4 (paperback)

Devolution in the
United Kingdom

Books in the Politics Study Guides series

Contents

Boxes

Tables

Preface

Since political devolution came onto the mainstream agenda in 1997 it has been a subject which has fascinated both academics and students of politics alike. Students are now learning that many aspects of their own lives, which in the past were almost identical with their contemporaries across the United Kingdom, are now sometimes radically different. On issues ranging from health and education to the attempts to deal with global warming, the devolved governments often deal with them in many differing ways. It is therefore unsurprising that political devolution is and will remain a key topic on any politics syllabus for as far as anyone can see. Students should also note that devolution is a constantly changing subject and, whilst much can be gained from reading this book, they should also keep their eyes and ears open as to the changes that are frequently occurring in both Westminster and all of the devolved bodies.

Both Dr Russell Deacon and Dr Alan Sandry have very much enjoyed the opportunity to write this text. We trust the reader will be able to gain as much from it as the authors have been able to. Both authors would like to thank Duncan Watts for commissioning the book in the first place, Nicola Ramsey and Eddie Clark from Edinburgh University Press and Neil Curtis for copy-editing. Dr Sandry would like to thank Jill, Thomas and all his family and friends for their support and inspiration along the way. Dr Russell Deacon would also like to thank his wife Tracey Deacon, daughter Alex Deacon and colleagues Anne Brooks and Steve Belzak for their support in the writing of this book.

CHAPTER 1

The Background to Devolution

Contents

Overview

Since the election of the Labour government in 1997, the semi-codified 'British constitution' has undergone one of its biggest changes in its history. The creation of a Scottish Parliament and assemblies in London, Northern Ireland and Wales have established major alternative centres of power to the Westminster Parliament itself. This first chapter defines the concept of devolution and examines the rationale behind it. The problems and drawbacks of devolution are also examined. The notion and importance of 'culture', and its influence on national identity are also explored.

Key issues to be covered in this chapter

- What is devolution? And its arrival on the United Kingdom's general political agenda
- How the political parties in Britain view devolution
- The rationale behind devolution and its drawbacks
- The main constitutional organisations or agreements that bind together the new devolved bodies
- What culture has to do with the concept of devolution

Introduction

The twenty-first century has started with a decade in which devolution on a Britain-wide level is seeking both to prove that it can be a success and that it can evolve models of democratic institutions. As these new devolved institutions have bedded in and are now coming into their elected third terms, British governmental processes are beginning to get to get to grips with this new form of devolved government. The opportunity for government policy and institutions to develop independently of the government in **Westminster** has increased significantly, and the traditional centralism of the British unitary state has started to dissolve around the edges.

The development of devolution

The *Penguin Dictionary of Politics* defines **devolution** as the 'process of transferring power from central government to a lower or regional level'. Over the course of the last century various governments established widespread administrative devolution. This involved the establishment of governmental departments such as the former Scottish and Welsh Offices. Political devolution, however, at a regional or national level, with the exception of Northern Ireland, did not arrive until 1999.

The rationale for and against devolution

One of the most common questions asked about political devolution is: why is it necessary? During the various referendum campaigns on devolution in Britain between 1997 and 2004 the rationale for and against it was made clear. The major reasons are given below.

The major advantages of devolution

It is the wish of the majority. In the **referendums** held in London, Northern Ireland Scotland and Wales, devolution was seen to be the will of the majority who voted. Subsequent opinion polls have shown that the majority of the population still desires a form of devolved government in these regions.

*Maintaining the **Union**.* In 1922 the failure to allow (**Home Rule**) devolution for Ireland earlier led to the separation of Southern

Ireland (Eire) from the rest of the United Kingdom. These separatist pressures in Northern Ireland, Scotland and Wales can be relieved by allowing a greater degree of devolution within each region.

It acknowledges distinct identity. Devolution acknowledges that the regions of the British Isles have differences and allows them to be developed. It also encourages the media to examine and to report on the world of politics outside of London and be aware that London is not always the centre of the political world.

It allows for fairer political representation. Over the last fifty years the people in Northern Ireland, Scotland and Wales have never elected a Conservative majority in a general election. Yet, for much of this period, they were governed by Conservative governments, elected by the majority in England. Devolution avoids this to a degree by allowing the majority party or parties elected in each devolved country's body to govern that country. It also provides a more proportional form of electoral system which better represents the way people vote.

The growing importance of the regional voice in the European Union. Most of the regions within the European Union already have their own devolved assemblies or parliaments. The European Union has evolved to allow these regional bodies to take part in the decision-making process, in such bodies as the Committee of the Regions. Devolution allows the various nations and regions within the United Kingdom to develop their own voices in a 'Europe of the Regions'.

Strategic planning. Certain functions, such as economic development and tourism, are too large for local government to deal with effectively by themselves. Devolution allows these to be carried out at a regional level.

A regional tier of administration already existed. Prior to devolution there were already government departments for Northern Ireland, Scotland and Wales. Their public administration had largely been devolved, and devolution provides greater democratic accountability.

It lifts some of the burden from Westminster. The Houses of Parliament are already over-congested with legislation. There is little time for effective scrutiny of primary or secondary legislation there. Devolution allows the nations and regions to spend greater time scrutinising or shaping legislation to suit their own circumstances.

The major drawbacks of devolution

During the devolution campaigns a number of drawbacks with the process of devolution was also highlighted.

Devolution was not the will of the majority but only the will of the majority of those who voted. In Scotland, Wales and London less that half of the population endorsed devolution. The combined majority either voted 'no' or did not vote at all.

It adds more fuel to the separatist flames. While devolution can be used to ease the demands for separatism, it is as far as most people want to go, and it may still encourage others to call for full independence. After the Labour Party, the nationalist parties are the second most powerful political parties within Scotland and Wales. The national assemblies and parliament allow them to enjoy a stronger voice politically.

Devolution could lead to a greater variation in standards of public-service delivery. To guarantee equal provision of services, such as welfare or health provision, across the United Kingdom it is sometimes better that all services are provided nationally. Allowing devolution for these could lead to inequity in overall provision within Britain.

Devolution costs money. The cost of the new buildings of government, together with salaries and with the running costs of the new devolved bodies, mount up to hundreds of millions of pounds. The new buildings for the Welsh Assembly and the Scottish parliament chambers have been mired in controversy.

There are too many politicians. People living in the regions with devolved government are now represented by as many as five different layers of government (town council, county council, regional assembly or parliament, Westminster Parliament and European Parliament). There is a danger that there will be:

- confusion over who deals with what, both inside and outside of the layers of government;
- 'buck passing' of responsibility between the different layers;
- 'turf wars' over who has responsibility for different layers of government;
- conflict between the layers of government resulting in chaos over the provision of services.

Devolved government will result in new political élites being formed who use the system to further the aims of their group at the expense of others.

These arguments for and against devolution regularly resurface as the United Kingdom continues to evolve its political structures.

The road to devolution

Towards the end of the nineteenth century and beginning of the twentieth, the issue of devolution was referred to as 'Home Rule'. The Liberal support for 'Home Rule' in Ireland led to interest in the same for Scotland and Wales. In 1885 the government established a Scottish Office. From then onwards there was a steady move towards further devolution, and this is explored in the following chapters of this book. Modern devolution can be linked mainly to that period, beginning with the rising tide of nationalism in the 1960s, which led the Labour Prime Minister, Harold Wilson, to set up in 1968 the Royal Commission on the Constitution under Lord Kilbrandon. Its remit was to 'examine the present functions of the central legislature and government in relation to the several countries and regions of the UK'. In the event, however, the Commission failed to reach a consensus, and came up with six alternative schemes and a minority Memorandum of Dissent. This might have ended matters if it were not for the fact that, in order to stay in power, the Wilson–Callaghan Labour government (1974–79) was dependent up on support from Plaid Cymru, the Scottish National Party (SNP) and the Liberals. The price of their support was the legislation on devolution. Both of the devolution referendums in Scotland and Wales failed (see chapters 5 and 7) and devolution did not therefore arise in this period.

Devolution remained subdued in Scotland and Wales for the majority of the 1980s. At a local level, the Conservatives began to reduce devolution, in areas such as housing and education, by taking away powers from local government. Their powers were transferred either to central government or to new quangos. The Conservatives also abolished some tiers of local government entirely, such as the Greater London Council and the metropolitan counties in 1985.

The Conservative government under Margaret Thatcher, who had always rejected devolution, dismissed calls for political devolution as 'the slippery slope to the break-up of the United Kingdom'. A similar position was taken by John Major. Only a few minor steps were taken to appease nationalist sentiment in Scotland and Wales.

The setting up of the Scottish and Welsh Select Affairs Committees and the strengthening of the role of the Scottish and Welsh Grand Committees were the major elements of enhancing those nations roles at Westminster. The Conservatives, however, remained committed to allowing devolution for Northern Ireland which they regarded as having 'special circumstances' owing to the troubles, both violent and political, which occurred then.

As the Conservative Party always remained against devolution, it meant that any breakthrough on this issue would have to involve the Labour Party. The other political parties, such as the Liberal Party and nationalist parties, remained too politically weak at Westminster to affect this issue in their own right. After the defeat of the referendums on devolution in 1979, which split the Labour Party in Scotland and in Wales into pro and anti camps, devolution became something of a non-issue while the party was led first by Michael Foot and then by Neil Kinnock. Although Kinnock did advance the cause in Scotland, it proceeded at a snail's pace in Wales. Neil Kinnock had been one of those most opposed to devolution in Wales. It was under John Smith, a long-standing supporter of devolution, who succeeded Kinnock in the summer of 1992, that the devolutionary cause was given a massive boost. Smith put the issue of a Scottish Parliament and a Welsh Assembly firmly in the forefront of government policy. After his death, he was succeeded by Tony Blair who then altered devolution policy by:

- ensuring that the world of business had a far greater say in the devolution proposals: for instance, the power of the Scottish Parliament to 'initiate some form of public ownership' was removed from the Scottish Conventions 1990 scheme;
- a commitment to hold referendums on the devolution proposals in Scotland and in Wales – this caused great anger in Scotland;
- forcing the Welsh Labour Party to include an element of proportionality in the elections to the Assembly, something that upset 'old' Labour elements within Wales;
- eliminating most of the dissent within the Labour Party concerning the devolution proposals and subsequent referendums.

Shortly before the 1997 General Election, Robin Cook (Labour) and Bob Maclennan (Liberal Democrats) signed the *Partnership For*

Britain's Future document; it became known as the Cook–Maclennan pact on constitutional reform. It was a document that stated that both the Labour and Liberal Democratic parties agreed constitutional principles for the forthcoming elections. Both political parties agreed to support the Labour Party's devolution proposals should Labour win the General Election. This meant that, for the first time, both parties were united behind devolution for Scotland and Wales. The Blair government, therefore, went into the election with an ambitious programme of constitutional reform. Once in power, to the surprise of many of their critics who doubted their devolutionist credentials, New Labour set about a radical programme of devolution within the United Kingdom (see Box 1.1).

Within months of Labour coming into power, two referendums were held to determine whether or not the peoples of Scotland and Wales wished to see political devolution within their respective countries? Although both countries voted 'yes', the result in Wales was on a knife edge, with a majority of just 0.6 per cent in favour of devolution. The Westminster-initiated Neill Commission on the Funding of Political Parties (1998) expressed some concern over the British referendum campaigns on devolution. In particular, it was concerned at the backing that the pro-devolution (yes) camps received from the

---

Box 1.1 Constitutional acts establishing or developing a devolved Britain

Referendums (Scotland and Wales) Act 1997
Government of Wales Act 1998
Scotland Act 1998
Northern Ireland (Elections) Act 1998
Regional Development Agencies Act 1998
Greater London Authority Referendum Act 1998
Greater London Authority Act 1999
Political Parties, Elections and Referendums Act 2000
The Regional Assemblies (Preparations) Act 2003
Planning and Compulsory Purchase Act 2004*
Government of Wales Act 2006

* strengthened planning powers of the English regional assemblies.

Box 1.2 A new department for a new era: the Department for Constitutional Affairs (DCA)

On 12 June 2003 the Labour government established a new government department to co-ordinate its modernisation of the British constitution, including those areas connected with devolution. The department's aim 'is to provide for effective and accessible justice for all, to ensure the rights and responsibilities of the citizen, and to modernise the law and constitution'.

The department is headed by the Secretary of State for Constitutional Affairs who is also jointly the Lord Chancellor (senior legal member of the judiciary, parliament and the government). The Department for Constitutional Affairs has control over the Scotland and Wales Offices in terms of the pay and administrative support for each. It is expected that, over time, both of these offices will be drawn more directly into the DCA.

government while the anti-devolution (no) organisations struggled to generate the finance to support their campaigns. It was felt, particularly in Wales, that if the 'no' camp had had more resources, the outcome of the eventual ballot would have been affected in their favour. As a result of this concern, the Political Parties, Elections and Referendums Act 2000 allows state funding for both 'official' sides in devolution referendums.

The political positions of the parties on devolution

How devolution develops in the future depends very much on how the winning political party (or parties) at Westminster feels about the whole concept of devolution. The political parties in the United Kingdom each has a different opinion on what political devolution should actually mean. These are described below.

From the mid-1970s to the late 1990s, the Conservatives were totally opposed to political devolution outside of Northern Ireland. They were united against devolution in their 1979 and 1997 Scottish and Welsh devolution referendum campaigns. In the 1980s and 1990s, the Conservatives concentrated power in Whitehall and Westminster, taking it away from local government. With the exception of an assembly for Northern Ireland, they consistently rejected calls for devolution within the United Kingdom. John Major described it as the 'break-up of the United Kingdom'. In the Welsh and Scottish referendums on devolution in 1997 their members supported the No campaigns. After the referendum on devolution resulted in a 'yes' vote, the Conservatives accepted it and have now committed themselves to making devolution work. They participate in the new forms of devolved British government. Some Conservatives' enthusiasm for devolution is now greater than that of the Labour Party. In Scotland, for instance, the party has pushed for further powers for the Scottish Parliament on taxation and, in Wales, some Conservative members of the Welsh Assembly are now publicly requesting the establishment of a law-making parliament. At heart, however, the party remains deeply sceptical of advancing devolution.

The Labour Party has been officially in favour of devolution for much of its recent history, although, in the 1979 devolution referendum, the party was split over the issue. At that time many powerful Labour voices, including future Labour leader Neil Kinnock, campaigned against the concept of devolution. During the late 1980s, however, the party as a whole, became more pro devolution. By the time of the 1992 General Election the party was committed to the restoration of a regional tier of government for London, and to the establishment of a parliament for Scotland and an assembly for Wales. Under John Smith, the plans for devolution became more cogent and part of Labour's manifesto for the 1997 General Election, and they were then implemented under Tony Blair. Since the 2001 General Election, the Labour Party has publicly supported the new devolutionary developments. Only in the English regions were there further attempts by the Labour Party to allow more devolution but, here, the concept of democratically elected assemblies has been rejected by the electorate. The party remains opposed to the establishment of any more law-making or tax-raising parliaments such as the one in Scotland.

The Liberal Democrats have been advocating devolution within the United Kingdom for longer than any other party. They have been committed to devolution for more than a century, and they were enthusiastic backers of it in the 1979 and 1997–8 referendums. They would like to see a law-making and tax-raising Welsh Parliament as well as regional governments with provision for their own primary law-making powers throughout England. The Liberal Democrats' policy is for the establishment of a federal state within the United Kingdom, with state and regional parliaments, and a federal parliament in Westminster, similar to the structures of government in Germany, Spain and the United States.

The nationalist parties in Britain (Plaid Cymru, the Scottish Nationalist Party) see devolution as a way to 'self-government' in Wales and independence in Scotland. Although, in the referendums, they supported the proposals for devolved bodies in their own countries, they would like to see further referendums through which they could achieve their own separatist agendas.

Tying devolution together

Across the United Kingdom and Northern Ireland political institutions are altering their structures to take account of devolution. In Westminster some of the select committees and parliamentary question times have been changed so that they no longer concern themselves with the activities of the devolved bodies. Members of Parliament have also had to get used to the fact they can no longer deal with issues, such as health and education, which are under the remit of the assemblies and the Scottish Parliament.

As well as the once- or twice-yearly meetings between ministers from the devolved executives and the government in Westminster, there are two further key elements that are involved in the working relationship between Westminster and the devolved governments. These are described below:

There is a Concordat and Inter-Departmental Concordats between the devolved bodies and Westminster and Whitehall. These are in the form of a document known as the *Memorandum of Understanding*. It puts the relationship between the assemblies, the Scottish Parliament and Westminster into a formal, but not legally binding, framework. It deals with matters such as the Joint Ministerial Committee, European policy and international relations.

The British-Irish Council or Council of the Isles. Membership of this consists of representatives of the British and Irish governments, the devolved institutions, the Isle of Man and the Channel Islands. It meets at summit level twice a year and in specific sectoral groups on a more regular basis. Its main task is to 'exchange information, discuss, consult and use best endeavours to reach agreement on co-operation on matters of mutual interest within the competence of the relevant Administrations'. The council meets for plenary sessions twice a year, a regular programme of sectoral meetings and *ad hoc* meetings as required. The first meeting of the British-Irish Council took place in London on 17 December 1999 and the council has been meeting regularly ever since.

British cultural identity and devolution

The notion of culture is deemed to be important in the context of devolution because it is at the very backbone of the nation state. In November 2000 the Welsh Assembly's Post-16 Education Committee affirmed the first definition of cultural identity. It stated that:

> Culture 'consists of all distinctiveness spiritual and material, intellec-tual and emotional features which characterise a society or a group' . . . Culture is about identity, history, diversity, education, traditions, symbols, language, innovation and shared experiences . . . A definition of culture as synonymous with the arts is inadequate and can lead to an exclusive interpretation of culture and create barriers in achieving a creative society for the many as opposed to the few.

British-Culture, therefore, can be seen in the wider context described above. That other definition of culture, concerning an appreciation of the arts and associated with those people or organi-sations connected with art, music, literature, libraries, broadcasting, film, museums and galleries, is a more tangible representation of culture and informs and supports the first. Each government within the United Kingdom has a minister (secretary) who is responsible for supporting this area of 'culture' within his or her respective nation.

The development of British culture

The Romans referred to the British mainland as a Britannia. After they left the island in AD 410, the terms 'Britannia' and 'Britain' were seen as of historical importance for more than a millennium. When the Scottish king, James VI, gained the throne of England and Wales in 1603, upon the death of the heirless Queen Elizabeth I, he was proclaimed 'King of Great Britain'. With the Union of the parliaments England and Scotland in 1707, the new nation became officially known as the United Kingdom of Great Britain. It already had a new flag, the Union Flag. The flag had been ordered by the Admiralty in order to end the practice of flying the flags of St Andrew and St George from the mast. To fly two flags also signalled a military engagement and Admiralty wanted to end this confusion. Scotland and England each wanted its flag to take precedence and, until Victoria's reign, both nations flew different versions of the flag, with their respective cross at the front. The Irish were still not in the Union but the flag would be adapted for them (to include the cross of St Patrick) when they joined a century later. The Welsh, as a 'mere principality', had no part in the new flag. To this day, the flag remains the most potent symbol of British identity but it has become associated with the political far right despite attempts by the mainstream political parties to 'claim it back'.

The 'culture and values' from the British Isles have spread widely from the sixteenth century onwards, and Britain started colonising various places across the world. Many of these 'culture and values' have been shaped by Anglican Christian tradition. At the same time, the ruling monarchs from James I onwards were keen to use the 'glue of Britishness' to keep their kingdom together. During this early sixteenth- and seventeenth-century colonial period, the 'culture' of Britain, as opposed to its constituent nations, was also defined. Surprisingly, these definitions of Britishness came, not from England, but from Scotland. In 1740, for instance, the Scots were so keen to be seen as part of the growing British Empire that the Scottish poet, James Thomson (1700–48), wrote the song *Rule, Britannia!* The song expressed Britain's desire to rule the waves, and the notion of a united Britain. Britannia and its form were initially most vigorously encapsulated in Scotland but, later on in the nineteenth century, it was promoted by the English ruling classes seeking to use its image as a counterbalance in international trade to the strength of France. At the same time as this was happening in Scotland, Ireland and Wales's cultural identity and nationalism were developing into their modern-day forms. Britain, it has been argued by the historian Linda Colley, was therefore a multi-nation state which was bound together during the course of the eighteenth and nineteenth centuries in three main areas:

1. In defence against other nations such as 'Catholic' France.
2. The common project of the British Empire.
3. Its shared Protestant religious and cultural traditions.

This new United Kingdom of Great Britain had created in the British Isles a borderless free-trade area, run by a single government and with a single currency, well over a century before the arrival of the European Union. The vision of a Great Britain and Empire as a trading block, promoting its own version of the Protestant work ethic across the world, was not always seen by many political theorists, particularly those on the ideological left, as a benign entity. Marxist theorists saw it as being merely a smokescreen used by operation of capital (business) to pursue the economic objectives of Empire. The peoples of the separate nations across the United Kingdom were caught up in the Marxist notion of 'false consciousnesses'. This meant that the subjects of these nations were, in fact, the subjects of colonialism but believed themselves (falsely) to be among the colonisers. As part of this 'false consciousness', British subjects endorsed the symbols and cultural aspects of Britain and Empire, such as monarchy, music, literature and theatre. They saw that this nationalistic British cultural identity in the late nineteenth century was being channelled into the maintenance of a cohesive British imperial cultural identity, rather than enabling the development of a cultural distinctiveness for the individual nations that made up the British Empire.

The main flaw in the notion of 'false consciousness', with respect to culture, is that it ignores the possibility of people sharing two or more cultures where they are not in conflict with one another. Thus, many of the population in Scotland, Wales, England, Ireland, or in English regions, such as Yorkshire and Cornwall, are happy to share British culture with their own more local cultures provided it does not suppress them. This duality of culture is at the heart of 'Britishness'.

Whether or not the Marxist notion of cultural identity has any true validity, it was evident that, in many areas of cultural life, the

Box 1.3 What shapes our culture and values?

There are many factors that shape our culture and values. The foremost are:

Education and academia: from nurseries to universities.
Music: from rock music to folk music.
Art: from sculpture to oil painting.
Sport: from rugby to netball.
Politics and ideology: from village hall to European Parliament and sharing the same monarch.
Literature: from biography to novel.
Language: from dialect to non-English mother tongues.
Shared history: from opposing the Romans to supporting the European Union.
Religion: from the Scottish Kirk to Muslim Council of Britain.

various nations within Britain had also absorbed culture and values from: each other, from one of the many nations they had colonised, or from the home nations of the various monarchs and their consorts that ruled them. With the end of the British Empire, the nationalism and the cultural identity associated with it, severely weakened British cultural identity thereby allowing the **Celtic fringe** and the regions of England to emerge from the shadow of Britannia and develop once more their own cultural identities. This cultural development meant that, as well as their own deep-rooted cultures, each nation within the United Kingdom also developed an eclectic mix of other nations' cultures. These cultures are still being shaped today (see Box 1.3).

Despite the fact that academics, historians and politicians often find it difficult to agree on what a specific nation's or region's culture and values can be defined as, what is generally agreed is that few people outside of England feel any real sense of British identity, feeling instead to be closer to the constituent nationalities they live among! Polls regularly suggest that, when asked, people feel themselves more often to be 'More Scottish or Welsh than British'. These nations, in turn, seek to define their own cultures and values. There has, therefore, been much written about what has happened to

Box 1.4 The end of Britishness?

Britishness was shaped from the nineteenth- and twentieth-century values of Empire, war and religion detailed earlier by Colley. Since the start of the twentieth century, however, Britishness as a cultural identity has been undermined by many events and cultural changes. The academic, Anthony Heath, noted that this was for a number of reasons:

1. The loss of Empire accompanied by a loss of influence as Britain ceased to be a global power.
2. The decline in the role and status of the Protestant religion in daily life.
3. The end of World Wars I and II which both brought the British nation together against a common foe.
4. The post-war economic decline that saw the end of Britain as a major manufacturing nation.
5. The end of British uniqueness in some areas, as parliamentary democracy, civil liberties and welfare states spread across the Western world and then further afield.
6. The rise of Welsh and Scottish nationalism which weakened the general sense of Britishness.
7. The move towards further European integration and Britain becoming a European nation.
8. The globalisation of the media with the subsequent dominance of American 'culture and values' diluting those of the British.
9. The decline of the role of the monarchy as an institution that binds the nations together.

culture in Britain after the end of 'Britishness' (see Box 1.4). In the following chapter we will examine what they believe the old and the new notions of culture to be in devolved Britain.

Conclusion

The arguments behind political devolution ran hot and cold throughout much of the late nineteenth and twentieth centuries. They divided not only political parties from one another but also caused divisions within the parties themselves. Sometimes, this caused parties to split, as it did with the Liberals over Home Rule in Ireland; at other times, it just meant that factions within each party supported different outcomes in any referendums held on this issue.

Although political and administrative devolution did occur before the election of a Labour government in 1997, it was limited to events in Northern Ireland and local government. It is the New Labour government that has started a radical process of devolution within the United Kingdom. At the same time, the cultures and values of these nations are also being reshaped. It is this process of continued devolution in England, Scotland and Wales, and its subsequent development, which are explored in the following chapters.

• •

✔ What you should have learnt from reading this chapter

- That devolution is both a contemporary and an historical political concept. Administrative devolution covers all British regions, political devolution is limited to the Celtic nations and to London.

- There are a number of clear democratic and cultural reasons for political devolution.

- Devolution also has a number of potential flaws concerning a lack of effective accountability when things go wrong, such as with the building of the new devolved institutions' legislative buildings.

- The events that have led up to political devolution, post-1997, began in the nineteenth century but it was not until 1997 that political devolution finally came to be widespread across the United Kingdom.

- The three main British political parties have traditionally had differing stances on political devolution. The Conservatives opposed devolution; the Labour Party opposed, then supported it to a limited degree; while the Liberal Democrats are the most supportive.

- The nationalist parties in Wales and Scotland support independence for their respective nations. Those in Northern Ireland either support joining the Irish Republic or staying within the United Kingdom.

- Cultures and values form the backbone of political devolution. Identifying cultures and values, however, is not always a straightforward process.

✎ Glossary of key terms

Celtic fringe Those nations within the United Kingdom who are direct decendants of the Celtic tribes of Northern Europe and who consider that Gaelic is, to a greater or lesser degree, their native spoken language.

Devolution The process of transferring power from central government to a lower or regional level.

Home Rule The term given to political devolution in the nineteenth and early twentieth centuries.

Quango An acronym standing for quasi-autonomous non-governmental organisation, also known as non-departmental public body (NDPB).

Referendum A vote given to the people on a set question; for example, do they wish to 'establish a law-making and tax-raising parliament'. If the majority of voters votes 'yes'; or if the vote exceeds the specified threshold (for example, 40 per cent of the total electorate) then the institution will be established.

Union The name given the 'union of nations' that makes up the United Kingdom of Great Britain and Northern Ireland (England, Northern Ireland, Scotland and Wales).

Westminster The location of the British Houses of Parliament in London, and the generic name often used to refer to the British Parliament.

Likely examination questions

You may not feel ready to answer these questions fully at this stage in the book but these are some examples of questions that may be asked:

Compare and contrast the differing views of the main three British political parties on devolution for England, Scotland and Wales.

To what extent is it true to say that devolution will lead to the 'break-up' of the United Kingdom?

Illustrate the key political events that led to the establishment of political devolution under the New Labour government of 1997.

Helpful websites

http://www.britishirishcouncil.org/ Details on the current and previous work of the British-Irish Council.

http://www.ucl.ac.uk/constitution-unit/ London's University College Constitution Unit's devolution programme, which is suitable for most chapters in this book.

http://www.lifeintheuktest.gov.uk/ The 'Britishness Test' (Life in the UK Test).

http://www.devolution.ac.uk/ The Economic and Social Research Council ran a large-scale research project from 2000 to 2005 on 'Devolution and Constitutional Change Programme' which covers all of the areas within this book.

Suggestions for further reading

V. Bogdanor, *Devolution in the United Kingdom*, Opus, 1999.

L. Colley, *Britons: Forging the Nation*, 1707–1837, Vintage, 1996.

J. Curtice, *Devolution and Britishness*, *ESRC Devolution and Constitutional Change*, Briefing No. 35, August 2005.

N. Davies, *The Isles,* a History, Macmillan, 1999.

R. Deacon, *Devolution in Britain Today*, Manchester University Press, 2006.

P. Dunleavy, A. Gamble, R. Heffernan and G. Peele, *Developments in British Politics*, Palgrave, 2004.

T. Gardiner, *The Cultural Roots of British Devolution*, Edinburgh University Press, 2004.

N. Groom, *Union Jack*, Atlantic Books, 2006.

A. Heath, *Is a Sense of British Identity in Decline?*, ESRC Devolution and Constitutional Change, Briefing No. 36, August 2005.

D. Robertson, *The Penguin Dictionary of Politics*, 2nd edn, Penguin, 1993.

CHAPTER 2

'Devolution All Round?' The Case of England

Contents

Overview

In terms of land size, population, economic and political power England is the largest country within the British Isles. Devolution within the British Isles has therefore only been possible with the will of the English. Yet England itself is not one homogeneous nation. Most towns, cities and county councils have developed their own cultural and geographical identities. At the same time, regional identities have developed, sometimes to the extent that people's loyalty and identity are more closely associated with their locality's identity than with that of the English nation state. In this chapter we will examine the development of English devolution. We will also assess the cultural significance of English nationalism.

Key issues to be covered in this chapter

- The origins of the concept of political devolution in England
- The extent to which the political parties have adapted to regional devolution in England
- How perceived cultural values are connected to concepts of 'Englishness'
- The other British nations' views of English cultural values
- The origins of modern devolution in England
- The emergence of English regionalism
- The Labour Party's evolving attitude to English devolution

The roots of English devolution

English regionalism was called the 'dog that didn't bark'. This meant that, unlike the other movements for political devolution in the British Isles, the movement for devolution in England was present but not very vocal.

At the beginning of the twentieth century, the creation of a parliament for England or separate parliaments for the English regions was considered as a partial solution to demands for Irish home rule. At the **Speaker's conference** in 1920 this 'Home Rule all round' was considered but rejected. Lloyd George tackled the Irish problem separately, creating parliaments in Dublin and Belfast, and, with the disappearance of the Irish problem from British politics, the proposals for English devolution were dropped for most of the rest of the century.

English cultural identity

Of all of the nations that make up the United Kingdom, it is the English that are happiest to see themselves as British rather than English. In 2004 some 51 per cent of those in England felt themselves to be 'British', while only some 38 per cent thought themselves to be 'English'. In Northern Ireland, Scotland and Wales, only 41 (2003), 19, and 27 (2003) per cent respectively of the populations felt themselves to be British. It seems that those who don't live in England are far surer of their own national identities.

Therefore, we must ask the question, what is Englishness? What does it mean to be English? The answers are as varied as they are numerous. The Conservative government minister, Norman Tebbit, once defined the notion of Englishness as being down to which cricket team one supports. Those who supported England were, as a result, 'English'. This simplistic 'Cricket Test' was not widely endorsed. This is not only because the 'England, cricket team is actually an 'England and Wales' cricket team, but also because the test ignores multiculturalism in England. Here, many nationalities are quite happy to integrate into English life in other ways but wish to continue to support the cricketing team of their birth or ethnic origin. They therefore have the same duality of nationality as those who consider themselves to be both English and British.

It is therefore not surprising that the English often look enviously upon the Scottish and the Welsh for being able to demonstrate their cultural identities so overtly through flags, national dress, anthems, and patron saints. For the English the most obvious symbol of nationality is the flag of St George. This is a red cross on a white background and has become associated with the English football fan, the far right British National Party (BNP) and the anti-European, right-wing party, the United Kingdom Independence Party (UKIP). This has meant that the mainstream political parties have tended to be wary of making overt use of the flag of St George and have been reluctant to embrace English nationalism in most respects. England's success in sporting events, such as the winning of the 2003 Rugby World Cup or the winning of the Ashes (cricket, although this was also technically shared with Wales) in 2005, or even the run-up to the 2006 football World Cup, have resulted in widespread benign use of the flag of St George. These are sporting occasions during which politicians were also glad to wrap themselves in the English flag.

There is also a number of fringe political parties that now identify themselves either directly with English or with regional identities. Meibion Kernow (Sons of Cornwall) is perhaps the most successful regional political party. Supporting independence for Cornwall and the strengthening of the Cornish language and cultural identity, it has been able to gain elected members to the county council, and has been in operation for a number of years. On a national scale, the English Democrats Party has built upon the desire for a separate English identity as, through devolution, the Celtic nations have re-established theirs. The party not only campaigns for an English Parliament and a national holiday on St George's Day but also seeks to ensure that English culture remains dominant over the 'multiculturalism' that has resulted from immigration. The English Democrats Party has not been electorally successful, however, and has no representation; it is therefore the media, particularly the tabloid press, who are the main identifiers of what they perceive to be English culture (see Box 2.1).

English culture has also been challenged, and to some extent altered, by large-scale post-war immigration. This is true to a much larger extent than is the case in any of the Celtic nations. In some

Box 2.1 How do the English like to view their cultural values?

English culture tends (where it is defined) to be:

- Based on Christian heritage and virtues, particularly those associated with the Church of England.
- Based on the landscape and evolution of its countryside: the village green-church-pub image portrayed in literature and in the idealised views of politicians.
- A respect for the traditions of England and an avoidance of sudden change. The support for the monarchy, the continuance of the class system and the peculiarities that go with the Houses of Parliament are evidence of these.
- Honesty and a respect for the law – 'an Englishman's word is his bond'.
- Belief in 'fair play', 'playing the game', 'good sportsmanship' and many other attributes that come from the national summer sport of cricket.
- Fairness and tolerance. That other cultures can be tolerated or even shared provided they do not conflict too severely with English culture.
- The provider of wealth for the less fortunate nations whether this be overseas or within the United Kingdom.
- The centre of, and trend setter in, world culture such as music and the arts, from Punk to the mini-skirt, and from the composer Edward Elgar to the artist John Constable.
- Built in part from the varying English regions with their more clearly defined cultural values going to create a 'greater whole'.

parts of England, such as the city of Leicester, the immigrant population is now larger than the native 'English' one. In some cultural areas, such as English cuisine, there has been a remarkable shift towards the new cultures. Chicken tikka masala is now the most popular dish in England, out-performing English culinary traditions such as fish and chips and roast beef. The contradictions of defining English culture mean that the English are not always viewed in the same light by others as they see themselves in (see Box 2.2).

Box 2.2 How are notions of English culture viewed by others?

- Intolerant of other cultures and values, wishing to remain the dominant player who calls all the shots.
- Not one nation but a collection of 'warring tribes' – those in the north disliking those in the south; those in one county or area disagreeing with, and not trusting, those in another.
- Jealous of the political devolution occurring throughout the United Kingdom but at the same time not having the self-confidence to establish it for itself.
- Failing to find its post-imperial values. The English have lost an empire but failed so far to find a new role.
- 'Little Englanders' who are conservative, xenophobic, anti-immigrant and stubborn when dealing with other nations or new things, such as introducing the Euro or embracing the concept of a European Union
- Dominated by class – a nation where who your parents are or where you went to school or university counts for more that what you studied and your own personal achievement.
- Lacking any real examples of cultural identity, with the possible exceptions of morris dancing and the maypole.
- To be hypocritical in their own demands for the preservation of 'English culture', complaining about cultural dilution while frequenting Indian and Chinese restaurants, indulging in salsa dancing, and taking all of their vacations abroad.

The embryos of devolved government

The Great Depression of the 1920s led to the Special Areas Act and the first steps towards regional policy. It was administered in a top-down fashion with policy coming from Whitehall and being delivered locally.

A comprehensive system of regional government for the United Kingdom, including England, came during World War II. Britain was divided into twelve regions under the direction of Regional Commissioners of Civil Defence. At the war's end, these regions formed the basis of the eleven Treasury standard regions used for the collection of statistical data. Other government departments, however, did not use them and, therefore, the use of these areas remained limited.

In the 1960s the Labour government under Harold Wilson set up, under their National Plan, the Regional Economic Planning Councils and Regional Economic Planning Boards in the English regions. These were nominated bodies composed of local government leaders, local business and trade union representatives and other people such as academics. They had no resources of their own and their role was limited to advising on planning and economic issues. Margaret Thatcher scrapped them in 1979 and few people seemed to even notice or care about their demise.

The 1980s was a comparatively barren time for English regionalism and devolutionary politics in Britain generally. The Labour governments of the 1970s had passed devolution acts for Scotland and Wales, and had considered the possible implications for England in a White Paper. The defeat of the devolution proposals in referendums in Scotland and Wales in 1979, however, and the defeat of the Labour government in the same year buried regionalism and devolution in Britain for almost two decades.

The Conservatives under Margaret Thatcher were opposed to government intervention in the economy, and this opposition extended to regional policy which declined under the Conservatives during the 1980s and 1990s. They also deeply resented the fact that the largest units of local government, the Greater London Council (GLC) and the six English metropolitan authorities, were controlled by the Labour Party and functioned as regional platforms from which to campaign against their own policy agenda. As a result of these clashes, the GLC and the metropolitan counties were abolished in 1986, and the powers of local government were curtailed in a series of measures and parliamentary acts during the Conservatives' period in office. Increasingly, the government bypassed democratic local government altogether, establishing special centrally controlled and funded bodies to perform important tasks such as the private-sector-led urban development corporations for urban regeneration.

From the late 1980s onwards, there was renewed interest in the regional level of government. The European Union's reforms to its structural funds (financial support to encourage economic development, emphasised the role of partnership and co-operation with local partners in drawing up bids for European funds, and it was argued that Britain, lacking a strong regional tier of government, was at a disadvantage in applying for European structural funds. Local authorities addressed these issues by combining into regional associations to discuss issues of common interest. Somewhat unexpectedly, the Conservative Manifesto in 1992 contained a pledge to create integrated regional offices in the English regions, combining the staffs and co-ordinating the work of four government departments – Trade and Industry, Transport, Environment and the Training, Enterprise and Employment Division of the Department of Employment – under one regional director. In 1994 the ten government offices of the regions or integrated regional offices (IROs) were established, with important functions of allocating the Single Regeneration Budget to local authorities and co-ordinating bids for EU funds and planning issues. To a limited degree, even the devolution-sceptical Conservatives had been persuaded of the practical merits of devolution for the English regions, although this was top-down 'executive regionalism' rather than the bottom-up 'local authority regionalism' which had been emerging through the growth of regional local authority associations based on a different eight standard regions. The IROs covered the ten regions of South-west, South-east, London, Eastern, West Midlands, East Midlands, Merseyside, Yorkshire and Humberside, North-west and North-east.

The emergence of English regionalism?

For much of the twentieth century the issue of devolution of power to the English regions remained something of a non-issue. In the last quarter of the twentieth century, however, the issue began to emerge. This was a number of reasons for this, as explained below:

Firstly, politicians from all parties and from local and central government have realised that a regional tier has functional advantages. Lobbying the European Union for more funding, for instance, is done more effectively if there are bodies to co-ordinate and represent the interests of local government, business and others at the European Union level. Increasingly, the European Union has come to favour a partnership approach to economic regeneration, and this is facilitated by regional structures where different interests can come together and reach a consensus on issues of common concern.

Secondly, other countries that were formerly unitary states, as the United Kingdom was, had previously undergone a process of region-alisation and the formation of regional structures. The record of regional government in other countries shows that it can confer bene-fits. Countries such as France or Spain, which followed this process, have claimed to have improved policy-making at the regional level by introducing devolved decision-making and have not sought to reverse the changes they have made.

Thirdly, during the 1990s, the first stirrings of regional movements in the English regions could be detected. There was some disquiet, however, that, though a regional tier of administration had emerged in the English regions since 1979, little of it was democratically accountable. There was pressure building to make these regional quangos more democratically accountable. A Campaign for a Northern Assembly in the north-east of England was established which conducted a 'constitutional convention' in that region, a similar body in the north-west and a campaign for a Yorkshire parliament were also started. In Yorkshire the cultural identity was much stronger than in many other areas; already, for instance, there is a Yorkshire day (1 August). These movements are small but have helped develop a debate on regional government and, initially, had some regional success within the Labour Party. This may be partly because, during its long period in opposition nationally (1979–97), often the only level at which the Labour Party remained successful and able to wield power was in local government, and a localist bias has now perme-ated some within the Labour Party.

Fourthly, some powerful figures within New Labour were person-ally committed to devolution. Key among these was John Prescott, Deputy Prime Minister. He had become aware of these regionalist feelings among some Labour members and had wanted some mea-sures for the English regions alongside the party's more ambitious proposals for Scotland and Wales. During the 1970s' devolution debates, some of the fiercest opponents of Scottish devolution in Westminster came from Labour's northern English backbenchers. They feared that a Scottish Assembly would divert resources away from the north of England. Labour certainly did not want those damaging splits to reoccur after their 1997 election victory, and so the party allowed some devolution for the English regions to creep on to its own political agenda.

The final reason that it was believed that the regions wanted more autonomy was the perceived success of administrative devolution in London, Scotland and Wales. The **political élites** within the regions across England became aware of the benefits of having a cabinet minister 'right at the heart of government to represent your interests' (as did Northern Ireland, Scotland and Wales). The English regions also saw that, through the **Barnett Formula**, the Celtic countries had received a greater share of public spending than they could have been getting. The regions were similarly impressed by the power of the economic quangos that represented these states, such as the Welsh Development Agency, which became very successful in attracting inward investment. The English regions therefore wanted to share in these benefits.

We should also note that the development of regionalism some-times has the affect of undermining politicians' attempts to create a wider English sense of identity. What takes precedence, for example, being a Londoner or Yorkshire man/woman or being English?

The Labour government and English regionalism

The Labour Party has been regarded as the party of the geographi-cal periphery because of its overwhelming political strength in Scotland and Wales. As such, it was thought to favour the interests of Scotland, Wales and the northern English regions. Historically, however, Labour sought to promote the interests of these regions by interventionist regional policy, not by creating regional parliaments or assemblies. It was committed to fulfilling socialist policies, such as the development of the NHS and the welfare state, on a national rather than regional scale. At the same time, the trade unions, working within the Labour Party, sought to continue with national negotia-tions concerning pay and conditions for the public sector rather than looking for any regional variations. Regional government would encourage the opportunity for disparities over wages and working conditions to occur within the public sector, and the trade unions were determined to prevent this.

During the 1960s and 1970s, Labour governments developed, and then expanded, regional-development grants to encourage firms to locate in more depressed regions and create employment in those places. Such regional policy was top-down and directed money from the centre to the regions. More locally based strategies were adopted in Wales and Scotland in the 1970s with the creation of the Welsh Development Agency and the Scottish Development Agency in response to challenges by nationalist parties in those countries.

In England, Labour's thinking is less well developed. In opposition, John Prescott had established a Regional Policy Commission which recommended the establishment of a regional development agency (RDA) in every region on the lines of the successful Scottish and Welsh Development Agencies. It also suggested they should be made accountable to the elected regional chamber. The regional chambers would be indirectly elected bodies bringing together regional stake-holders such as local government, business and environmental groups. It was also envisaged that these indirectly elected chambers might, in time, become directly elected regional assemblies. This proposal was enthusiastically adopted by John Prescott, then shadow Minister for the Environment and became party policy. Jack Straw, as shadow Home Secretary, developed the proposals for regional chambers in the New Labour Party document *A Choice for England*. The regional chambers would initially be indirectly elected bodies composed of local government and regional business representatives, and possibly drawing in figures from other areas, such as further or higher education. They would be responsible for planning issues, preparing and co-ordinating bids for European regional funds and other economic issues.

In office, Labour implemented devolution for Scotland, Wales and Northern Ireland with energy, dedication and persistence. In the shape of the former superministry the Department of the Environment, Transport and the Regions (DER), it created for the first time a minister responsible for the English regions. Its approach to the English regions was somewhat more leisurely. After the 1997 General Election there was a lot of discussion about how regionalism would develop within England. Would it have a number of mini-assemblies like that planned for Wales? When the Labour government came into power, it decided after only six weeks to legislate for regional development agencies (RDAs) and not regional chambers. By April 1999 the RDAs were established, accountable to government ministers. These bring together the economic 'stakeholders' in the region to develop and direct European structural fund bids and other industrial and training policies. They have the status of non-departmental public bodies (NDPBs) – popularly known as quangos. These NDPBs are answerable only to the secretary of state and not to local government.

Jack Straw set a number of tests for the RDAs to move to elected chambers. They would have to petition to become a directly elected assembly. Parliament would have to legislate for this, and the electorate in the region would have to approve these measures in a referendum. These steps were described as a 'triple lock' on English devolution to ensure that unnecessary and unwanted tiers of government could not be imposed on unwilling regional electorates.

A fourth hurdle complicated the process of English devolution still further, however. Jack Straw maintained that, before regional chambers could be established, the two-tier system of local government across much of England (counties and district/borough councils) was turned into a system of unitary authorities (single-tier principal councils). This was because, when introducing another new layer of government, the central government wished to get rid of an existing one at the same time so as to not to overwhelm the public with too many layers. As there were only a few areas in England without both county and district councils, this was a very high hurdle to jump, and the unpopularity of further local-government reform (not least with local authorities themselves) made this hurdle higher still. Paradoxically, the imposition of a unitary structure of local government in both Scotland and Wales by the anti-devolutionist Conservatives enabled a smoother transition to devolution because the political complexities of altering local government structures could be avoided by the Labour government. With all these checks in place, it was clear that, whereas Scottish and Welsh devolution, were priorities for a future Labour government (and were among its first legislative acts after May 1997) English regionalism, outside of the capital, was placed firmly down the agenda.

While the elected Greater London Authority was established in 2000 the other eight English regions still did not have elected regional chambers. In May 2002, the government unveiled its policy on regional assemblies in the White Paper, *Your Region, Your Choice* and, in November 2002, the government introduced the Regional Assemblies (Preparations) Bill into Parliament. The bill enabled regional referendums to be held, but did not define the powers or functions of regional assemblies, which were defined later.

The ministry charged with undertaking English devolution was also going through a series of changes. The Department for the Environment, Transport and the Regions (DETR) was split up in 2001, after the general election, to form the Department for Transport, Local Government and the Regions (DTLR). In 2002, the DTLR was itself broken up, with the 'Transport' part going to form its own Ministry of Transport. The remaining sections were to be brought into the Office of the Deputy Prime Minister (ODPM), John Prescott, and put together with his existing related responsibilities for social exclusion and the regions (including the government offices in the regions). Later on, after a scandal involving an extramarital affair with one from his own civil servants, John Prescott had most of his powers stripped from him and, on 5 May 2006, under Ruth Kelly's leadership, most of his responsibilities went into the new Department for Communities and Local Government (DCLG). The development of the ministries dealing with English devolution seemed to be evolving much faster than the policy they were trying to deliver.

Local government and devolution

When the New Labour government established regional development agencies and regional chambers in the English regions, local government was brought on to the executives of these bodies. Unlike the regional economic planning councils of the 1960s, the RDAs had clearer functions and resources to fulfil them. Yet, at the same time, it was apparent that these bodies would take functions of local government if they were to evolve into elected regional chambers. In addition, as we stated earlier, for elected regional chambers to come into being, one layer of local government (either county or borough council) would have to be abolished to introduce a single tier of local government. Few local councils looked forward with any eagerness to the possibility of being scrapped. This made the notion of elected regional councils an unpopular option among most local authorities in England.

Conclusion

For most of the twentieth century, the idea of political devolution for the regions in England was overshadowed by the devolution occurring elsewhere in the United Kingdom. Then, in 1997, the Labour Party created regional development agencies and regional chambers in the English regions that have revitalised the nature of government in the United Kingdom. The establishment of the RDAs was seen by some as the start of a process of English devolution that will eventually match that occurring in the rest of Britain. Others, however, wanted the establishment of the RDAs to be an end in itself.

••

What you should have learnt from reading this chapter

- England is the dominant partner of the nations that make up the United Kingdom but is the weakest in terms of its own devolved governmental development.

- English devolution has a history stretching back almost a century.

- English cultural identity is a difficult concept to define, it has also often been associated with racism and far-right political nationalism.

- English regionalism has been developing over the last fifty years and, to some extent, undermines English culturalism and national identity. This regionalism has become a central plank in Labour's own devolution policy.

Glossary of key terms

Barnett Formula Set up in 1978 in preparation for devolution, it is used to share out public expenditure between the countries of the United Kingdom based on relative population size. The government updates the Barnett formula annually using mid-year population estimates.

Political élites Those politicians or administrators who are at the heart of the policy-making and/or power process

Speaker's conference A conference involving all of the members of the British Empire and Commonwealth parliamentary speakers. They are held to discuss matters of international importance.

? Likely examination questions

Illustrate the extent to which it is true to say that English devolution has been more a case of 'evolution than revolution'.

To what extent does English culture define English political identity? In your answer examine the key constituents of English culture.

Helpful websites

www.englishdemocrats.org.uk English Democrats Party: a political party that campaigns for an 'English Parliament and the restoration of English cultural values'.

www.englishindependenceparty.com English Independence Party: details publications which examine English culturalism.

www.ucl.ac.uk/constitution-unit The Constitution Unit, University College, London produces regular reports on devolution in England.

http://www.devolution.ac.uk/ The Economic and Social Research Council ran a large scale research project from 2000 to 2005 on 'Devolution and Constitutional Change Programme' which covered many aspects of devolution in England. Its website contains further details on English devolution.

Suggestions for further reading

R. Body, *England for the English*, New European Publications, 2001.

R. Deacon, *Devolution in Britain Today*, Manchester University Press, 2006.

S. Heffer, *Nor Shall My Sword: The Reinvention of England*, Phoenix, 1999.

CHAPTER 3

English Devolution: 'London' Leads the Way?

Contents

Overview

The development of English devolution has been rapid since 1998. The Greater London Assembly and London Mayor have come into existence, as have regional development agencies and the English regional assemblies. These developments were in part aimed at redressesing the imbalance caused in the English regions by devolution occurring elsewhere in the United Kingdom. This chapter therefore examines how English devolution could help fill some of the devolutionary gaps occurring across the United Kingdom and how, in turn, Westminster has dealt with English devolution. The desire for the English regions to gain further autonomy is examined with respect to the devolution referendum in the English North-east. The chapter finishes by exploring the most prominent area of English devolution – the Greater London Assembly and the personality politics that surround its mayor, Ken Livingstone.

Key issues to be covered in this chapter

- The arguments for and against English regionalism
- The role of regional development agencies and regional assemblies
- The regional referendum on an assembly in the English North-east, and the reasons for its failure
- How Westminster is adapting to English devolution
- The way in which the London mayoral candidates are selected and the method by which the public elects them to office
- The development of the Greater London Authority under its mayor, Ken Livingstone, and its perceived successes and failures

Introduction

We saw in the previous chapter that the practical application of devolution had started to spread throughout England after 1997. Although this was a stated aim of the New Labour government when it came into power in 1997, sceptics believed that English devolution outside of London would be left to 'wither on the vine' politically as it would prove to be too politically contentious to get off the ground. In the event the Labour government, spurred on by its pro-devolutionary Deputy Prime Minister, John Prescott, used the period towards the end of its second term to test the extent to which the public in England was in the mood for more devolution.

The evolution of English devolution

Devolution in England lacked many of the clear-cut certainties of the devolution occurring elsewhere in Britain. When it came into power in 1997, the New Labour government's establishment of the **regional development agencies** (RDAs) was seen in policy terms as putting into place the 'raw building materials out of which some kind of English devolution might be created'. From their inception, however, the agencies were seen as suffering from some major flaws (Box 3.1).

We should note, however, that the RDAs and the **regional assemblies** (RAs) do provide the regions with the benefits of devolutionary power, such as closer and more realistic economic and government planning and development, which is more sensitive and focused

---

Box 3.1 The arguments against English regional development agencies

- Few people are sure of what they do.
- Their management structure is 'top-heavy and unaccountable'.
- Their budgets are only 1 or 2 per cent of the budgets of the Scottish Parliament or Welsh Assembly, despite the fact that, in a number of English regions, the per capita gross domestic product was far higher than in these nations.

on the region in question. They can also help foster a sense of identity, which is important in economic development and regeneration, and the application and implementation of European Union funding.

Under the Regional Development Agencies Act 1998, Deputy Prime Minister John Prescott established a political level to oversee the RDAs to try to solve some of their problems. The political level was known as the regional chambers, commonly referred to as 'assemblies', and came about in 2000.

In 2000 the British Social Attitudes survey showed a mere 18 per cent of the population favouring regional devolution for England while 62 per cent wanted the status quo. In some areas, such as Merseyside, the North-west, and Cornwall and the South-west, it was felt that there was greater demand for regional devolution. Therefore, delegates to Labour's 2001 election national policy forum agreed that the party had to recognise the 'legitimate aspirations of the English regions', and belief was expressed in the idea that elected regional assemblies might well be the next step in Labour's programme of constitutional reform. In May 2002, the White Paper, *Your Region, Your Choice*, was published and detailed plans for English devolution. The regional chambers were to be slightly enhanced versions of what already existed, but with larger budgets and more powers of scrutiny. This disappointed the English pro-devolutionists as these strategic powers and limited budgets were far inferior to their own inspirational role model – the Welsh Assembly. The other key point of the White Paper, however, was that no region would gain an elected regional chamber unless it was endorsed in a referendum. In May 2003 the Regional Assemblies (Preparations) Act was passed which detailed what regional assemblies would do, but they were still seen as having a number of drawbacks (Box 3.2).

The North-east says 'No'

On 4 November 2004 the 1.9 million electors of the North-east voted on whether they wanted to have an elected assembly and, at the same time, what form of single-tier local authority they wished to see for their area. These two questions had been asked as a result of a culmination of the Labour government's English Regionalism programme. The referendum campaign in the North-east had brought

Box 3.2 Responsibilities and problems of the English regional assemblies

The English regional assemblies have been designed to implement regional strategies for:

- Sustainable development
- Economic development
- Skills and employment
- Spatial planning
- Transport
- Waste
- Housing
- Health improvement
- Culture and tourism
- Biodiversity

The problems with regional assemblies

- There is a financial cost to expanding a layer of government 'bureaucracy'.
- There are the practical problems associated with the restructuring of government, including matters such as confusion over service delivery, disruption and risk of failure.
- There is a constitutional uncertainty over the role of the assemblies in their relationships with Westminster.
- The regional assemblies can deal directly with the European Commission, thus bypassing Whitehall and Westminster and furthering the establishment of a 'federal Europe'.

forward two opposing sides. Professor John Tomaney led 'Yes 4 the North East' which included Labour and Liberal Democrat parties and some prominent supporters, such as the president of Newcastle United FC, Sir John Hall, and the sports commentator and former Olympic athlete Brendan Foster. Though an MP in the neighbouring region, Deputy Prime Minister John Prescott became known as the main political spokesman for the Yes camp.

In the actual campaign the Yes camp promoted the message that the vote was all about establishing identity, with slogans such as 'be proud, vote yes' and 'this is your chance, don't waste it'. The facts that the North-east could enjoy some of the benefits of the devolved nations and that this would bring political decision-making away from London to the North-east were also highlighted. The Yes camp also attempted unsuccessfully to link the official No campaign directly with the Conservatives and the BNP and other right-wing parties which were alien to most traditional Labour voters.

'The North East Says No' (NESNO) campaign was under the chairmanship of John Elliott, a former Conservative candidate who enjoyed a lot of business and Conservative party support. As a result of Elliott's past links, the No campaign became synonymous with the Conservatives. This was the official group backed by the Electoral Commission. In addition to NESNO there was also another No campaign, the 'North East No Campaign' run by Neil Herron and backed mainly by UKIP. Both No campaign groups constantly argued with each other but this did not have an impact on their overall message. The message was that a new assembly would be a waste of money. To this effect they produced a slogan 'politicians talk, we pay', which turned out to catch the public's mood in the North-east.

Although, initially, polls had indicated that the Yes campaign would win, as the campaign advanced, the numbers who said they were certain to vote, and would vote No, exceeded considerably those who would be voting Yes. The postal vote, over a period of weeks, as opposed to the traditional ballot-box voting on just one day, also meant that few voters left their vote to near the actual polling day and therefore could not be persuaded by the developing arguments of either side. On 4 November, when the results came in, some 77.9 per cent voted No and just 22.1 per cent voted Yes, on a turnout of almost 50 per cent. Every council area in the North-east voted No by more than two to one.

In the period after the North-east referendum, the Labour Party persisted with its commitment to RDAs and to regional chambers. This was partly because the party that the existing structures would be too difficult to remove. The Conservatives wished to scrap the RDAs and regional chambers, and the Liberal Democrats wanted to streamline them into agencies run solely by local councillors. It was the Labour Party, however, which won the 2005 May General Election and therefore it was their manifesto commitment to continue to develop the RDAs with further powers on planning, housing development and

Box 3.3 The lessons learnt from the North-east referendum for pro-English devolutionists

In March 2005 the Office of the Deputy Prime Minister Parliamentary Select Committee published the results of its investigations into the withdrawn, draft Regional Assemblies' Bill. There were lessons to be learnt for English pro-devolutionists. They were that:

- Any future assemblies should be given 'real' powers if and when on the political agenda.
- Any future legislation to set up elected regional assemblies in England needs to be more ambitious than the draft bill.
- The scope of the powers and responsibilities which the government was prepared to give assemblies was disappointing and would limit their effectiveness.
- Any further initiative to promote assemblies must be backed, and commitments made, by all government departments, not just the Office of the Deputy Prime Minister (ODPM).
- The role of local government, once an assembly was up and running in a region, had to be clarified.
- A clearer case is needed for elected regional assemblies in terms of value for money for the electorate.

transport, which will determine the short-term future of English regional devolution. The failed referendum, however, had produced some important lessons about the future of English devolution (see Box 3.3).

Westminster and English devolution

In 1998 the House of Commons Procedure Committee began an enquiry into the *Procedural Consequences of Devolution* with respect to England. When it reported back in July 1999, it set Westminster two questions to answer:

1. What legislation would continue to be debated at Westminster and what new procedures should there be for its scrutiny?
2. What would be the role of the territorial select and grand committees?

On a number of the devolved areas Westminster had already become a *de facto* English parliament. At the beginning of 2001 a survey conducted by the University College, London Constitution Unit showed that four select committees had already established an exclusively English membership. These were the committees dealing with the devolved matters of education, employment, health and home affairs.

The second question was also important for Westminster because, even before devolution, Scotland and Wales, whose affairs were dealt with by the Scottish and Welsh Offices respectively, had had their own select, standing and grand committees to consider all legislation for those territories. The Procedure Committee decided that it would be unfair to retain the Scottish, Welsh and Northern Irish Grand Committees if there were not some similar arrangement for English MPs, although England had over 500 members which made it totally impractical to have an English Grand Committee. Therefore, Westminster went back into its past and resurrected the defunct Standing Committee on Regional Affairs which looked at the English regions and which operated between 1975 and 1978, containing only eleven MPs. The committee first meet on 10 May 2001 but only really examined issues relating to the north of England and, consequently, it was regarded by most observers as something of a 'damp squib' as far as wider English devolution is concerned.

The governance of London

While it became apparent by 2004 that the English regions did not want regional government, the national capital, London, had already decided to take this route. London had already demonstrated it perhaps had the strongest sense of regional identity of all the regional areas in England. London's historical roots go back to the first century AD where it was established as a Roman town. Since then the town has expanded into a city of some 7.3 million (2003) with a strong sense of its own multicultural identity. Most of the inhabitants of this cosmopolitan city readily identify themselves as Londoners, adding to this sense of regional identity.

The events leading to the establishment of the Greater London Authority (GLA) began when the Greater London Council (GLC) was abolished by the Thatcher government in 1986. When that happened, it meant that London became the only major city in the developed world not to have some form of city-wide government. Instead, there was a confused system of public and private bodies that took over the duties of the old GLC. As the situation became more confused, politicians of all parties sought to bring back some form of city government. When John Major's Conservative government introduced their nine government offices (GOs) in 1994, one of these was the Government Office for London (GOL). Members of the Major administration, most notably Deputy Prime Minister, Michael Heseltine, then became enthused with the idea of a directly elected mayor for London, on the grounds that most major cities, such as Paris and New York, had one. The idea of an elected mayor also became popular within the Labour Party, as was the idea of a return of the GLC. Just a short while after winning the 1997 General Election, the New Labour government produced *New Leadership for London*, in July. This Green Paper suggested that there should be a directly elected mayor and an elected London assembly. In October 1997 the Greater London Authority (Referendum) Bill was introduced to Parliament in order to allow the population of London to decide on whether or not they wanted an elected mayor and assembly.

The 7 May 1998 referendum result appeared to be a resounding endorsement of the government's proposals, 72 per cent voting in favour and only 28 per cent against. The turnout of only 34.6 per cent of the electorate meant that only 23 per cent of Londoners had voted for the GLA, which gave it a somewhat limited electoral mandate. Despite the size of the mandate, the Greater London Authority Act of 1999 received the royal assent on 11 November 1999, and led to the mayoral and assembly elections of 5 May 2000. In these, Ken Livingstone, formerly a Labour MP who had been expelled from the party when he stood against the official Labour candidate, won by a considerable majority in an electoral system known as the **Supplementary vote** (SV) system.

In elections for the London assembly a different electoral system was used from the mayoral one. This was the Additional Member System (AMS) based on fourteen London constituencies and eleven London-wide seats. Neither in 2000 nor in 2004 did one political party gain a majority in the London assembly (Table 3.1).

Party	2000		2004	
	Constituency	List	Constituency	List
Labour	6	3	5	2
Conservative	8	1	9	0
Liberal Democrats	0	4	0	5
Green	0	3	0	2
UKIP (Veritas Party)	0	0	0	2

Table 3.1 London assembly election results, 2000 and 2004

Ken Livingstone rejoins Labour

In September 2002 Ken Livingstone applied to be re-admitted to the Labour Party but his application was rejected. Despite the fact that many at the top of the Labour Party didn't want Ken Livingstone back in the party in January 2004, the Labour Party National Executive Committee met and interviewed Livingstone, and then allowed him back into the party. The problem that there already was an existing Labour mayoral candidate, Nicky Gavron, was dealt with by offering her previous position as Deputy Mayor, in the post-election assembly.

In the 2004 mayoral election, turnout was slightly up on that of 2000, to 36.95 per cent, with almost 2 million people voting. Once again, Livingstone was the winner, albeit now back in the Labour Party.

The mayor and the London assembly

The London mayor was Britain's first ever directly elected executive politician. Politicians before this had been elected solely to represent a constituency as opposed to a particular executive post in governance. This provided the mayor with a powerful electoral mandate, in many ways more powerful even than that of the prime minister who is elected only as an MP. The mayor is held accountable by a number of devices, including the monthly report he must make to

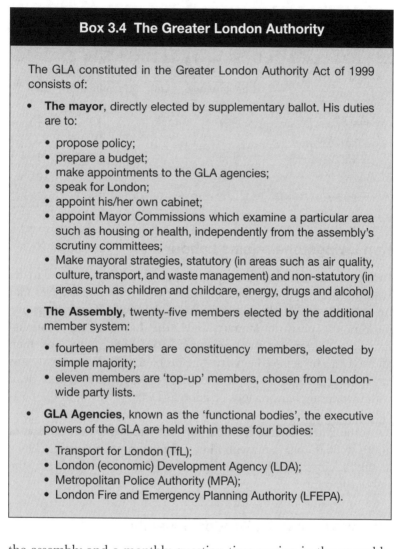

Box 3.4 The Greater London Authority

The GLA constituted in the Greater London Authority Act of 1999 consists of:

- **The mayor**, directly elected by supplementary ballot. His duties are to:

  - propose policy;
  - prepare a budget;
  - make appointments to the GLA agencies;
  - speak for London;
  - appoint his/her own cabinet;
  - appoint Mayor Commissions which examine a particular area such as housing or health, independently from the assembly's scrutiny committees;
  - Make mayoral strategies, statutory (in areas such as air quality, culture, transport, and waste management) and non-statutory (in areas such as children and childcare, energy, drugs and alcohol)

- **The Assembly**, twenty-five members elected by the additional member system:

  - fourteen members are constituency members, elected by simple majority;
  - eleven members are 'top-up' members, chosen from London-wide party lists.

- **GLA Agencies**, known as the 'functional bodies', the executive powers of the GLA are held within these four bodies:

  - Transport for London (TfL);
  - London (economic) Development Agency (LDA);
  - Metropolitan Police Authority (MPA);
  - London Fire and Emergency Planning Authority (LFEPA).

the assembly and a monthly question-time session in the assembly. Once a year, the mayor must present a progress report to the assembly which is then published as a 'State of London' address and debated by the assembly. Twice a year, in association with the assembly, the mayor speaks directly to Londoners in a 'People's Question Time'. From 2002 onwards, the Chair of the Greater London Assembly has also taken part in these sessions. The mayor also has the task of drawing up a budget that is presented to the assembly before the end of February each year. The GLA has tax-raising powers of its own, and it has access to the council tax precept which raised around half a billion pounds in 2003–4. In one way, this makes the GLA more powerful than the Welsh and Northern Ireland assemblies which have no tax-raising powers. The assembly can approve a budget by a simple majority but any amendment requires a two-thirds majority. The assembly also elects a chair and deputy chair who have the power to take over many mayoral functions in the mayor's absence.

The assembly is regarded by some as a 'toothless talking shop'. Its only real power is to reject the mayor's budget but, in a system of governance that is built on partnership, this issue hasn't really arisen. In addition, it has limited power over London's thirty-two borough councils and over the City of London regarding their decision-making, even when their powers overlap. With no substantial or legislative powers, the assembly has had to build up its scrutiny remit of the mayor's activities based on committees (see Box 3.5).

Box 3.5 Role and powers of the London assembly

It has nine committees involved in scrutiny and policy creation:

- Budget
- Commission on London Governance
- Economic Development, Culture, Sport and Tourism
- Elections Review
- Environment
- Health and Public Services
- Planning and Spatial Development
- Transport
- Standards

The mayor, however, need not take on board any committee recommendations and is also able to set up his/her own mayoral commissions if he/she wishes to enquire into any particular issue. This fact weakens the scrutiny role of the assembly's committee structure. The assembly does, however, have the power to appoint nearly all of the senior GLA staff, a power which some believe should go to the mayor.

The Livingstone administration

After May 2000, the governance of London was dominated by the personality politics that surrounded the new mayor, Ken Livingstone. The battle with central government over who controlled the London Underground, the congestion charge, the London bombings, and the worldwide contest to gain the 2012 Olympics dominated newspaper headlines in Britain and further afield. Despite the fact that, on occasions, the GLA's chair and the wider GLA itself tried to exert its power, it is the mayor who has come to symbolise, in many ways, the people of London.

Initially, Ken Livingstone took the middle ground as a politician. To the surprise of his many critics, he concentrated on law and order and supported the principle of 'zero tolerance' on criminal activity. By using his power to raise council tax for specific purposes, he increased the size of the Metropolitan Police by 1,050 officers. It was therefore through policing and public transport that Livingstone sought to define his first period in office. It was the congestion charge that was to be Livingstone's most controversial policy during his first period as mayor yet, despite fierce initial protest, it became a success that was studied throughout the world. While politically, Livingstone could be shrewd on some occasions, such as the setting of the price on the congestion charge well before the next mayoral election, on others he caused a great deal of negative publicity. This was most apparent on 4 February 2005 when, after leaving a party marking twenty years since the former Culture Secretary, Chris Smith, became Britain's first openly gay MP, he got into a fierce argument with a reporter, Oliver Finegold, from the *Evening Standard*. When Finegold insisted on questioning Livingstone, the following conversation occurred:

Mr Livingstone: 'Are you a German war criminal?'

Mr Finegold: 'No, I'm Jewish, I wasn't a German war criminal. I'm quite offended by that.'

Mr Livingstone: 'Ah right, well you might be, but actually you are just like a concentration camp guard, you are just doing it because you are paid to, aren't you?'

This exchange occurred a week after the sixtieth anniversary of the liberation of Auschwitz so it caused a large-scale public row over the mayor's insensitive remark. The Prime Minister Tony Blair, Culture Secretary Tessa Jowell, Transport Minister Tony McNulty, The Board of Deputies of British Jews, the London-wide Anti-Semitism Policy Unit, Deputy London Mayor Nicky Gavron, the GLA, Holocaust survivors, Jewish community leaders and numerous other organisations and politicians all called on Ken Livingstone to apologise. He refused and, though he apologised for causing offence to the Jewish community, he would not apologise to the journalist or to his newspaper, stating: 'If that is something people find they cannot accept I am sorry but this is how I feel after nearly a quarter of a century of their behaviour and tactics.' On 24 February 2006, the independent local government Adjudication Panel for England suspended Livingstone from office for one month, having found that he brought his office into disrepute when he acted in an 'unnecessarily insensitive' manner.

The whole affair indicated that, to a large extent, devolution in London revolved around one man, Ken Livingstone. It indicated the powerlessness of the GLA over the scrutiny of the mayor's actions, a lack of power that GLA members had been concerned about almost since the GLA's inception. To this extent, in its 2005 General Election Manifesto, the Labour Party indicated it would review the powers of the London mayor and GLA. No doubt the personality politics of London's devolution will feature predominantly in any such review.

Conclusion

On 10 March 2006, Lord Falconer, the Labour government's Constitutional Affairs Secretary and Lord Chancellor, declared at the ESRC Devolution and Constitutional Change Programme conference that the idea of ever having a parliament for England was a non-starter. He stated: 'To the idea of an English Parliament, we say: not today, not tomorrow, not in any kind of future we can see now. Devolution strengthens the union of the United Kingdom; English votes for English issues would wreck it.'

No other mainstream political party supported a single parliament for England either. Devolution at a regional level within England, however, is not quite so dead. Ironically, democratically elected devolution in England has been successful only in the English capital, London. The other regions of England, that were initially believed to have wanted greater autonomy from London and to have their own regionally elected assemblies, do not have this desire in sufficient numbers within their own populations. There are two main reasons why the English regions do not want devolution. Firstly, they do not have the cultural and historical cohesion of London. Secondly, there is a widespread antipathy towards creating 'more' politicians in any layer of government.

The devolutionary experiments in London, Northern Ireland, Scotland and Wales created some envy among regional MPs and councillors but not enough to cancel the negativity felt to the overrule concept of regional devolution. For the time being, however, the regional chambers (assemblies) and RDAs continue in existence, gradually evolving new powers. Their overall lack of accountability, which was meant to have been rectified by making the assemblies elected, has not occurred, neither have the local councils, Whitehall and Westminster been effective in making them more accountable. Outside of London, there remains something of a democratic deficit throughout the English devolutionary system.

. . . .

✔ What you should have learnt from reading this chapter

- That English devolution is a much weaker form of devolution than exists in the rest of the United Kingdom.

- Initially there was believed to be widespread public support for devolution in England but, when this was put to the test in the referendum in the North-east, the opposite was found to be the case.

- The failed referendum in North-east has meant that devolutionary policy in England is going through a new, slow period of evolution, the outcome of which is uncertain.

- One example of regional political devolution in England is in existence, the Greater London Assembly and London mayor.

- The GLA and its mayor have had a series of political successes and have been seen as role models on environmental issues, such as the 'congestion charge'.

- The personality politics which surround the London Mayor, Ken Livingstone, have meant that the GLA and the mayorship have become closely associated with the actions of just one man.

Glossary of key terms

Regional assemblies (RAs) The executive bodies that monitor the running of the RDAs. They include nominated politicians, business persons and community leaders. It is not directly elected.

Regional development agencies (RDAs) The administrative bodies that deal with devolved government in the English regions.

Supplementary vote (SV) system All voters are given a first and second preference when they vote. If no candidate gains 50 per cent of the vote on the first preference then the second preferences are counted and the candidate with the highest number of combined votes wins.

Likely examination questions

In the light of political devolution of Northern Ireland, Scotland and Wales, the Houses of Parliament are now sometimes described as being the 'English Parliament'. To what extent is this remark valid?

The road to further English devolution was halted with the referendum result in the North-east in November 2004. With reference to the reasons for the result, examine exactly what was wrong with the proposed devolution in England and how it might now progress?

Helpful websites

www.odpm.gov.uk/ The Department for Communities and Local Government is the government department responsible for English devolution.

www.london.gov.uk/ The Greater London Authority and London mayor's official website.

www.ucl.ac.uk/constitution-unit The Constitution Unit, University College, London produces regular reports on devolution in England.

http://www.devolution.ac.uk/ The Economic and Social Research Council 'Devolution and Constitutional Change Programme'.

Suggestions for further reading

M. Cole , 'The Changing Governance of London', *Talking Politics*, Summer 2000.

R. Deacon, *Devolution in Britain Today*, Manchester University Press, 2006.

T. Heppell and R. McCreanor, 'English Regional Governance: The Next Stage of Constitutional Change', *Talking Politics*, vol. 15, no. 3, April 2003.

P. Lynch, Toward an England of the Regions? Devolution and the Future Government of England, *Talking Politics*, vol. 16, no. 3, April 2004.

T. Travers, *The Politics of London: Governing an Ungovernable City*, Routledge, 2004.

CHAPTER 4

The Evolution of Scottish Devolution

Contents

Overview

Before any assessment of the current state of play within Scottish politics can take place, some background to the events leading up to the arrival of devolution within Scotland needs to be noted. Starting with the Act of Union in 1707, this chapter explores some of the developing themes within Scottish politics and then focuses upon the devolution referendums of 1979 and 1997. This will supply the required setting for explorations of the contemporary political scene in Scotland that will be looked at in chapters 5 and 6. Having assessed developments within England, we now move on to look at the case of Scotland within the governance of Britain as a whole, and the politics of Scottish devolution in particular.

Key issues to be covered in this chapter

- General political history of Scotland
- The demands for Scottish home rule
- Scotland's Devolution Referendums: 1979 and 1997
- The 'Yes' and 'No' Campaigns
- The Scottish Constitutional Convention
- Devolution at last!

Scottish political history: 1707 onwards

In historical terms, Scotland has always had an uneasy association with England, its sometime friend, sometime foe, south of the border. Things appeared to have settled to some extent in the early eighteenth century when, in 1707, Scotland was incorporated into the **Act of Union** with England and Wales. This Act of Union brought to an end the separate parliamentary systems that had been in existence in England and Scotland. The act led to the creation of a single parliament, based in London, that would cover the United Kingdom.

Nevertheless, Scotland did maintain its separate identity through the continuation, in part or in full, of its legal, clerical, financial, and educational institutions. While some politicians in London thought that Scotland would gradually assimilate itself into England, the fact that Scotland retained some of its pre-1707 administrative functions probably helped it to maintain its unique national identity at a time when some advocates of the Union began referring to Scotland as 'North Britain'. It is fair to claim, therefore, that, despite efforts to downplay it, a separate civic tradition of 'Scottishness' was much in evidence at this time.

Despite the occasional eruption of **nationalistic** sentiment since then, the relationship between the old adversaries has been fairly peaceful overall, and has ensured the existence of a general degree of political and social stability. As tensions mounted throughout the United Kingdom in the late nineteenth century, however, with a call for self-government from many people within the Celtic fringe, most notably in Ireland (though Scotland did have a small **'home rule'** movement), the **Scottish Office** was established in 1885, with a Secretary for Scotland, to supervise the administration of everyday life in Scotland. Prior to this, the home secretary had been the person responsible for overseeing Scottish affairs at Westminster. The task of the Scottish Office was to assume responsibility within Scotland for certain aspects of social policy. As the powers and tasks of the Scottish Office accrued over time, it branched out to include such areas as health, employment, agriculture, fisheries, and farming. Despite the deliberate tactic of Westminster not to overplay this development within Scottish governance, this restructuring of the political landscape amounted to the recognition that Scotland had a particular agenda in relation to these matters, and some specific, though limited, policy development within these fields was allowed by the British government. Added to this, the introduction, in 1907, of a separate Scottish Grand Committee at Westminster, Scottish 'over-representation', in terms of the number of MPs Scotland elected to the House of Commons in relation to the English ration of seats since 1922, and, since 1926, a seat for the Scottish secretary of state in the cabinet, could be portrayed as attempts by the British government to make the Scottish people feel that issues of concern to them were being taken seriously and to dampen any developing Scottish claims to independence.

Devolution, if not independence, had been raised as an option for Scotland and for Wales at various times in the late nineteenth century and around the time of the World War I, but this was mainly in connection with the implications of far-reaching constitutional change in Ireland. In 1924, George Buchanan, MP for the Glasgow Gorbals constituency, attempted to promote a Scottish Home Rule Bill at Westminster. It was swiftly dismissed as it was felt by Unionist politicians that any further change in the UK's political set-up at the time, in the wake of Ireland's departure, would have undoubtedly placed unbearable pressure on the unitary nature of Britain's constitution.

Growing pressure

The acknowledgement by Westminster that Scotland was a distinct geographical, if not fully political, entity did not, however, succeed in diminishing the enthusiasm of those seeking independence. The founding of the Scottish National Party in 1934 – during an era when the Scottish economy was being ravaged by the depression of the interwar years – helped further to propel these arguments on to the main stage of Scottish and British politics. Moreover, symbolic gestures, such as the removal by a group of nationalists of the ancient Stone of Scone from Westminster Abbey in 1950 (the stone on which Scottish monarchs were traditionally crowned), ensured that the issue of self-government did not fade from view. While public spending in Scotland reached an all-time high in the post-war period – according to official statistics some 20 per cent higher per capita than in England – there was still a noticeable level of resentment in

Scotland to the British political institutions. This was highlighted by the collection of two million signatures by the Scottish National Convention – formed in the 1920s and consisting mostly of MPs and local-authority representatives – supporting the idea of devolved government. The petition was presented to the Conservative government in 1952 but to no avail. Just prior to the petition's presentation, the Conservatives had set up a Royal Commission on Scottish Affairs and granted the Scottish Office an extra junior minister. Despite these moves, however, the Conservatives, being the most Unionist of all the Westminster-based parties, had little time for those people who called for Scottish home rule to be introduced.

By the 1960s there were signs of anger across Scotland as some English and foreign-owned companies started to lay off workers because of a downturn in the economy. Resentment across Scotland was also aroused as the British government chose to locate the Polaris submarine base on the Clyde despite a wave of local and national opposition. On the back of these events came the 'breakthrough' election victory of the SNP's Winifred Ewing at the Hamilton by-election of November 1967 which ensured that the topic of Scottish independence, or at the very least Scottish devolution, remained high on the political agenda. The effect of the rise in nationalist sentiment at this time is exemplified by the fact that, by 1968, even the Conservative Party, conscious of the unfolding mood of the Scottish people and keen to remove the potential sting of the SNP, proposed the establishment of a Scottish assembly. Edward Heath, Conservative Party leader and Prime Minister from 1970 to 1974, stated during his speech to the Scottish Conservatives' annual conference at Perth his intention to set up the assembly. Although Heath, when in power, was to renege on his promise, the official Conservative line was to commit to the idea of an assembly subject to the findings of the Kilbrandon Royal Commission on the Constitution. This had been established by Labour Prime Minister, Harold Wilson, in 1969, and it eventually reported in 1973. Nothing was done upon the commission's conclusion, however, and Margaret Thatcher, upon her installation as the new Conservative leader in 1975, swiftly adopted a hostile stance to any talk of diminishing the role of Westminster.

Added to all of the above, the discovery of oil and gas in Scottish waters, and the subsequent expansion of the allied industries that saw

Aberdeen and its hinterland experiencing an economic boom, enabled those advocating the break-up of the present constitutional arrangements to point to the fact that an autonomous Scotland would have no difficulty in paying its way in the modern world. This would be the message emanating from the 'It's Scotland's Oil' campaign in the 1970s, which argued for profits from the oil bonanza to be redistributed within Scotland itself.

The Labour Party and Scottish devolution

The Labour Party had traditionally been seen as being in favour of centralised political authority, with Westminster as the location for that authority. The rise of nationalism, and support for nationalist parties in Scotland and in Wales, in the late 1960s and early 1970s, forced the Labour Party into rethinking its position on the devolution of power. By September 1974 the government had published a White Paper entitled *Democracy and Devolution: Proposals for Scotland and Wales*. The White Paper envisaged a Scottish assembly with limited legislative powers. The new Scottish institution would be elected by the traditional first-past-the-post system and it would be funded by an annual block grant from the Exchequer in Downing Street. Labour took up the cause of devolution as a manifesto pledge and doggedly stuck with it up to the 1979 referendums in Scotland and Wales. Internal disputes within the Labour Party, however, meant that the case for devolution was never convincingly made. Nevertheless, it is not unfair to say that Labour's leadership supported devolution in an attempt to quench the rising flames of Scottish nationalism.

What was more divisive for the party was the fact that the Scottish Labour Party itself was not convinced about the proposals for devolution. The proposals for Scottish devolution proved problematic for some members who were keen on devolution because Labour's plan was that Parliament would retain the right to legislate on any matter devolved to the assembly, and the Secretary of State for Scotland would remain to advise Parliament on how to respond to Scottish assembly decisions. Hence, there was initially some confusion as to what tasks the assembly would undertake, and then there was a certain degree of disappointment that the proposals did not offer Scotland greater powers to make its own laws and policies.

After the rejection of the Scotland and Wales Act in 1977, a separate Scotland Act was eventually granted Royal Assent on 31 July 1978. The constitutional problems were threefold. First, devolution was very limited, arousing little general public enthusiasm. Second, there were to be different schemes for Scotland, Wales, and England, which raised the problem of variable treatment, symbolised in the '**West Lothian Question**'. This emerged because Tam Dalyell, the anti-devolution MP for West Lothian, questioned the logic that he could come down to Westminster, following the creation of a Scottish assembly, and continue to vote on legislation for England on issues which, in Scotland, would have been transferred to the Scottish assembly, and over which

---

Box 4.1 Why devolution? What was wrong with the Scottish Office?

The problems with the role of Westminster and Whitehall in the government of Scotland were:

1. The people of Scotland saw the Scottish Office as a London-based department that was often thought of as being too far removed from everyday life in Scotland.
2. As Westminster and Whitehall had to administer UK affairs, some people in Scotland said that Scottish matters were not being discussed enough in the Houses of Parliament.
3. The Scottish Office was seen by many to be ineffective during times when Scotland was suffering from high unemployment and economic crisis.
4. There was a growing belief, from about the 1960s onwards, that the Scottish Office would not be able to operate as the type of inclusive and democratic political forum that many people in Scotland desired.
5. In the 1980s opposition parties in Scotland kept reminding the Scottish people that the Scottish Office was being run by the Conservative Party which had only ten Scottish seats and less than a quarter of the Scottish vote.
6. The growing tide of regionalism and regional administrations within European politics led some people to ask whether rule by a few centrally based politicians was the way forward for Scottish politics.

English MPs would have no say. Dalyell argued that this was not constitutionally fair and he, accompanied by a group of English Labour MPs, mostly from the north of the country, set about trying to defeat the legislation. Finally, some of the ambiguous language that was used in the Scotland Act could have created a recipe for future political conflict between the seats of power in London and Edinburgh.

Scotland's first chance for devolution: 1979

The year 1979 saw devolution referendums in Scotland and in Wales to establish whether the Labour government's devolution proposals should be put into practice. On 1 March the Scottish people voted in favour of devolution by a small majority. 51.6 per cent had voted 'Yes' but this was only 32.8 per cent of the total electorate. A figure of 40 per cent of the total electorate voting had been set as a requirement before the proposals could be put into practice. This figure had been settled on through what became known as the 'Cunningham Amendment'. The name derives from its instigator, George Cunningham, a Scot who was Labour MP for Islington South and Finsbury, and who wanted to scupper the devolution proposals, believing that demanding a high level of electoral participation would put immense pressure on those advocating devolution to inspire the Scottish public to go out to vote for the devolution proposals. Cunningham saw his amendment passed in the House of Commons by 168 votes to 142. Therefore, the 'Cunningham Amendment' became embedded into the Scotland Act as Section 85(2).

When the votes came in, it became clear that this figure of 40 per cent of the electorate had not been reached. Therefore, the devolution proposals for Scotland, that had been set out by the Labour government under Prime Minister James Callaghan, could not be put into effect. This was seen as a severe blow, not just to the Labour Party who instigated the devolution proposals, but also to the nationalist cause in Scotland as a whole. There were also reprisals as accusations circulated claiming that devolution had been undone by the 40 per cent ruling, something unheard-of in British politics, where a simple majority was normally deemed sufficient. Post-referendum, the SNP wanted the Labour government to continue its commitment to implementing devolution in Scotland. When no such commitment was forthcoming, all eleven SNP MPs voted with other opposition parties during a 'no-confidence' debate in the House of Commons on 28 March 1979. The Labour government lost the vote by 311 votes to 310. The Labour government realised that its days were numbered. Labour/SNP relationships were further damaged as Labour politicians gave the SNP the label of 'Tartan Tories'.

The 1980s: devolution remains on the agenda

Despite the failure to enact the Scotland Act and Wales Act of 1978, and the subsequent political fallout, the devolution issue did not go away. Indeed, as the 1980s developed, opposition to many of the political decisions stemming from Westminster grew throughout Scotland. One major decision during this period that infuriated most people in Scotland was to use Scotland as a testing ground for a new form of local taxation that became known as the '**Poll Tax**'. In 1987 Prime Minister Margaret Thatcher announced to the Scottish Conservative Party Conference the arrival of the Poll Tax in which everybody was expected to pay the same amount regardless of their economic circumstances. Thatcher believed that introducing a flat-rate tax in the land of the free-market advocate, Adam Smith, would prove unproblematical. She badly miscalculated the mood and the political inclinations of the Scottish people, however. This became clear when opposition parties and pressure groups organised a 'Can't Pay, Won't Pay' campaign and there was talk of London politics being thrust on the people of Scotland. Tommy Sheridan, later to become a Member of the Scottish Parliament, went to Saughton jail for his part in the movement against the Poll Tax.

The subsequent failure of this tax system had two far-reaching effects so far as the people of Scotland were concerned. First, it was to bring about the demise of Margaret Thatcher's term as Prime Minster and, second, it reinvigorated the devolution debate across Scotland. To add to the Conservatives' problems, the Scottish Affairs Select Committee – set up in 1979 to review the work of the Scottish Office – did not sit after 1987 as there were not enough Scottish Tories to provide a majority. This led to political stagnation as commentators claimed that Scottish matters were not being given a proper hearing at Westminster. The Conservatives used to have a majority of seats in Scotland; indeed, at the 1955 General Election, they captured over 50 per cent of the Scottish vote. But this steadily declined and, by the time of the 1987 General Election, out of seventy-two Scottish seats, only ten Scottish Conservatives were elected. This led to talk of what was called 'The Doomsday Scenario'. The idea was that the Conservative government had no mandate to govern Scotland. Hence, some opposition politicians saw their political task to be as obstructive as possible until such time that the issue of an elected Scottish parliament or assembly was back on the cards.

The Scottish Constitutional Convention

With this as a backdrop, therefore, it was not a complete surprise when, after the 1987 General Election, the Campaign for a Scottish Assembly, that had been set up in 1979 in the wake of the first devolution referendum, decided to establish a **Scottish Constitutional Convention** to push for constitutional change. There was also a general feeling throughout Scotland, backed up by opinion polls (see Table 4.1), that the time was the right to reignite the devolution debate.

Table 4.1 MORI opinion polls on constitutional change, 1979–87			
	Independence	Devolution	No change	Don't know
March 1979	14	42	35	9
November 1981	22	47	26	5
March 1983	23	48	26	2
March 1984	25	45	27	3
February 1986	33	47	14	6
March 1987	32	50	14	6

Source: P. Lynch (2002), *The History of the SNP*, p. 243.

The convention was made up of a cross-section of Scottish political and civil society; though, for differing reasons, the SNP and the Conservatives took no part in the deliberations of the convention. The Scottish local authorities played a significant role, as did a wide range of organisations, from the Scottish Trades Union Congress and the Scottish Churches, led by Canon Kenyon Wright, to the Women's Forum Scotland and the Ethnic Minorities Communities, led by Pek Yeong Berry of the Racial Equality Council. The intention of the convention was to formulate plans for the smooth introduction of devolution to Scotland and to put pressure on the anti-devolution Conservative government that was in office at that time. Throughout its existence, the Scottish Constitutional Convention proved to be the bandwagon for constitutional reform, and its report, *Scotland's Parliament. Scotland's Right*, published in 1995, was widely seen as laying the basis for the devolution proposals that were adopted by the Labour government on taking office in 1997. What the convention also managed to do was to function as a channel for the 'new politics' that was being discussed at the time by people, such as social policy-makers, politicians and think tanks, all of whom wanted to promote wider representation through new democratic structures. As this 'new politics' included the promotion of regionalisation and devolution, the Constitutional Convention found itself with a series of allies who demanded social and political reform.

Yes or No: the Campaigns for and against devolution in Scotland

Campaigns for and against devolution were part of the political scene in 1979 and in 1997. They were designed to bring together people and organisations who strongly advocated one position in this debate. While the main Yes and No campaigns acted as umbrellas, under which different groups and individuals could shelter, there were also smaller party-led or organisationally based campaigns, such as the 'Conservative Yes Campaign' or the fascinating example whereby the Clydesdale Bank made a statement that asked their customers to support a No vote at the 1979 referendum. But the main impact came from the major Yes and No campaigns.

The Yes campaigns

By the time of the 1979 referendum, the 'Yes for Scotland' had been in existence for over a year. Launched in January 1978, it was designed to embrace people from across the political spectrum. It quickly attracted support from political activists, as well as from members of the Scottish clergy, media personalities, writers, and so forth. The Labour Party, however, did not climb on board as many of its members supported devolution because they viewed it as a form of accountable government, which Scotland needed, but were repelled by any talk of going further down the constitutional road and using devolution as a stepping stone towards a self-governing Scotland. Labour and the trade unions, therefore, came up with the notion of a 'Labour Movement Yes Campaign'.

In 1979, the SNP was generally supportive of the 'Yes for Scotland' umbrella organisation. Some SNP members also felt, however, that they needed their own group to put across the SNP message on Scotland's future political status. Hence, the SNP supporters were able to work within one or both groups as they sought to achieve a devolved institution.

By 1997 the Yes campaign had been greatly boosted by the high-profile activities of the Scottish Constitutional Convention. Hence, it could be argued that the umbrella 'Yes' organisation, 'Scotland Forward', had a relatively easy task in front of them. There were some internal tensions, however, and the No camp attempted to highlight any splits. Nevertheless, the Yes camp, despite some problems, helped to secure a clear victory in the devolution referendum.

The No campaigns

The key No campaign in 1979 was Tam Dalyell's 'Labour Vote No' movement. It was significant because Dalyell advocated a rejection of the devolution proposals by pushing his 'West Lothian Question'. The 'Labour Vote No' organisation was set up initially during a meeting of Labour MPs at the House of Commons. Another prominent supporter of 'Labour Vote No' was Brian Wilson, later to be a minister in the Scottish Office. Despite the media attention given to Dalyell and his objections to devolution, the larger No campaign was visible with the presence of the 'Scotland Says No' movement.

'Scotland Says No' was formed on St Andrew's Day in 1978. It offered a broad anti-devolution front that saw it gain support from across the political spectrum and enabled it to incorporate a host of organisations with suspicions about devolution. 'Scotland Says No' had a forerunner in the 'Scotland is British' campaign which had

---

Box 4.2 Who was involved in the Scottish Constitutional Convention?

Joint Chairs: Lord Ewing of Kirkford and David Steel MP
Chair of Executive Committee: Canon Kenyon Wright
Scottish Members of Parliament
Scottish Members of the European Parliament
Local authorities
Political parties

- Scottish Labour Party
- Scottish Liberal Democrats
- Social Democratic Party
- Co-operative Party
- Democratic Left
- Scottish Green Party
- Orkney and Shetland Movement

Scottish Trades Union Congress
Scottish Churches
Federation of Small Businesses
Women's Forum Scotland
Ethnic Minorities Communities
Forum of Private Business
Campaign for a Scottish Parliament
Law Society/Faculty of Advocates
An Comunn Gaidhealach
Comunn na Gaidhlig
Committee of University Principals
Scottish Council for Development and Industry

played up the advantages of Scotland being part of the Union. While both organisations claimed to appeal to anyone interested in opposing the devolution proposals, in reality, the majority of those interested in securing a No vote in any referendum were Conservative supporters. Also, the fact that some senior Scottish business people, and Scottish businesses, supported 'Scotland Says No' tended to isolate anti-devolutionists who saw themselves on the political left.

Matters had changed to some extent when it came to the 1997 referendum. The No movement faced a huge uphill battle and their 'Think Twice' campaign was launched at Murrayfield Stadium by the staunch Unionist, Donald Findlay. Though it was judged to add character to the debate, its ultimate failure to convince Scotland not to 'sleepwalk' into devolution probably said more about the mood for devolution of the Scottish people than it did about the lacklustre argument against its implementation.

The push for devolution: 'Top-down' or 'bottom-up'?

What needs to be asked about these calls for devolution is whether they were '**top-down**' initiatives or '**bottom-up**' demands. The argument that they were 'top down' arises because devolution, being a change in a country's constitutional set-up, requires the coming together of politicians with legal and constitutional experts in order to construct proposals for change. It is sometimes said by opponents of devolution that it is a 'chattering-class' issue that does not find any real support among people on the ground.

The alternative viewpoint, the 'bottom-up' argument, claims that there is a widespread demand for constitutional change among the electorate at large. The contention here is that there is a grass-roots sentiment in favour of political change. The 'bottom-up' position holds that the Scottish people were unhappy with the arrangements of the Union, as they stood, and they were therefore enthusiastic that some changes were enacted.

It is probably fair to conclude that both the 'top-down' and 'bottom-up' positions have their merits. Proposals for devolution have to be arranged by politicians, legal experts and constitutional advisers. So, an element of 'top-down' planning and implementation is required. In the case of Scottish devolution, however, it is clear that a substantial degree of 'bottom-up' enthusiasm for devolution was in evidence. This showed itself in opinion polls, prevalent grass-roots attendance at rallies and public meetings, and the majority vote when it came to the devolution referendums.

Devolution arrives: 1997

In the devolution referendum held on 11 September 1997 the Scottish electorate was asked to give its approval to two proposals. On the first matter of establishing a Scottish parliament (Question 1) 74.3 per cent voted in favour. On the second matter of awarding the parliament the right to have the power to vary the basic rate of income tax (Question 2) 63.5 per cent voted in favour (see Table 4.2 below for the full figures).

Devolution at last!

After decades – some would say centuries – of campaigning and lobbying, Scotland finally secured devolution after the 1997 referendum. New political institutions were to be established and Scotland's relationship with the rest of the United Kingdom would be altered. In the following chapter the ways in which these changes have affected the governance of Scotland and what the political map of Scotland now entails will be covered.

Table 4.2 Scottish Parliament referendum results, 1997			
		Votes cast	Percentage
Question 1	Agree	1,775,045	74.3
	Disagree	614,400	25.7
Question 2	Agree	1,512,889	63.5
	Disagree	870,263	36.5

Box 4.3 Important events on the road to a Scottish parliament

- 1707: The Act of Union between Scotland and England does not resolve every political question.
- 1885: The establishment of the Scottish Office.
- 1934: The SNP is formed with the aim of campaigning for an autonomous Scottish political system.
- 1960s–70s: Growing confidence among nationalists, and public discussion about devolution.
- February 1978: Passing of the Scotland Act, paving the way for devolution.
- 1 March 1979: First devolution referendum proves to be unsuccessful in ensuring devolution is up and running.
- 1989–95: Scottish Constitutional Convention campaigns for a Scottish parliament to be established.
- 1 May 1997: Labour government elected with a commitment to hold another referendum on devolution.
- 11 September 1997: Second devolution referendum ensures Scotland has its own parliament.
- November 1998: The Scotland Act, laying out the provisions for devolved rule, receives Royal Assent.
- 6 May 1999: First elections to the Scottish Parliament.
- 12 May 1999: First sitting of the new Scottish Parliament.
- 1 July 1999: The Queen officially opens the Scottish Parliament.

What you should have learnt from reading this chapter

- The 1707 Act of Union did not settle constitutional matters in Scotland once and for all.

- The Scottish Office was established in 1885 to try to ensure that Scottish issues were seen to be given greater priority at Westminster, and to offset calls for independence.

- The views of the Labour Party and the Conservative Party about Scottish devolution have fluctuated over time.

- Critics of devolution, such as Tam Dalyell, opposed the introduction of devolution as they maintained that, once in place, it would be irreversible.

- The Scottish Constitutional Convention enabled a democratic dialogue about devolution to take place, and its findings enabled a smooth period of transition for devolution in Scotland.

- Although a majority of people in Scotland wanted devolution, it was only secured after the second devolution referendum in 1997.

Glossary of key terms

Act of Union The legal political union between Scotland and England (and Wales) in 1707. Sometimes referred to as simply as 'the Union'.
'Bottom-up' devolution The idea that devolution is a key demand of the electorate which organises itself in movements to petition for it.
Home rule The demands of a people to control their own social, political and economic affairs. Calls for home rule usually stem from internal pressure but sometimes external groups may also push for self-government.
Nationalistic Being supportive of a nation and promoting the causes of that nation in a political and cultural sense.
Poll tax Short-lived experiment by the Conservative government of Margaret Thatcher to introduce a flat-rate local income tax, known as the 'community charge' or 'poll tax'. During a bitter political period at the end of the 1980s, it was eventually defeated by 'people power' and a campaign of non-payment.
Scottish Constitutional Convention An independent campaigning group made up of a cross-section of Scottish society that included, among others, MPs, representatives from various political parties, members of trade unions and church leaders.
Scottish Office Set up in 1885 and administered by a secretary of state for Scotland who is a member of the UK cabinet. The Scottish Office's powers have been curbed since the introduction of devolution and the arrival of the Scottish Parliament.
'Top-down' devolution The contention that the idea of devolution was conjured up by politicians and other groups, like the judiciary, and was forced on to the people of Scotland (and Wales).
West Lothian Question The conundrum, first raised by Tam Dalyell, whereby Scottish MPs – and in some cases Welsh MPs – can vote in the House of Commons on English matters while English MPs have no say on matters devolved to the Scottish Parliament (or the Welsh Assembly).

? Likely examination questions

Did the 1707 Act of Union bring an end to Scottish desires for self-government?

Was the setting up of the Scottish Office in 1885 seen as a way of playing down Scottish calls for independence?

Discuss the ways in which the discovery of oil in waters off the Scottish coast boosted the arguments for Scottish devolution?

How influential was the Scottish Constitutional Convention in securing devolution for Scotland?

Helpful websites

Scottish political history is covered on links at the following sites:

www.ukpol.co.uk

http://dir.yahoo.com/Government/

http://dmoz.org/Society/Government/

http://britannia.com/history/

Suggestions for further reading

V. Bogdanor, *Devolution in the United Kingdom*, Oxford University Press, 2001.

C. Harvie and P. Jones, *The Road to Home Rule*, Polygon, 2000.

I. G. C. Hutchison, *Scottish Politics in the Twentieth Century*, Palgrave, 2001.

Scottish Constitutional Convention, *Scotland's Parliament. Scotland's Right*, 1995.

B. Taylor, *The Road to the Scottish Parliament*, Edinburgh University Press, 2002.

CHAPTER 5

The Governance of Scotland

Contents

Overview

While Scotland has always managed to maintain and keep up some uniquely Scottish institutions since the 1707 Act of Union, effective political governance of Scotland by the Scottish themselves was not one of them. This chapter looks at the governance of Scotland since the first Scottish parliament elections in 1999. It looks at the wider system of government in Scotland and, in so doing, shows how it is not just the Scottish Parliament and the Scottish Executive that control political affairs in Scotland.

Key issues to be covered in this chapter

- The Scottish Parliament
- The Scottish Executive
- The committee system
- The Scottish Parliament and Europe
- Local government in Scotland
- The quangos and devolution

The Scottish Parliament: its role and functions

The **Scottish Parliament** is the only institution in the United Kingdom, bar the Westminster parliament, that can make its own original legislation. This means that it has primary legislative powers, often referred to as '**primary legislation**', across a number of policy areas. Primary laws, as distinct from secondary laws, are those that originate, and are then turned into legislation, from one source – that is, the Scottish Parliament. Devolved Scottish issues can therefore be raised and scrutinised at Edinburgh without having to have recourse to Westminster. These devolved matters include areas such as education, agriculture, local government, health, environment, sport and the arts, economic development and home affairs (see Box 5.1). The Scottish Parliament also has control over many facets of transport policy.

Box 5.1 Devolved government in Scotland

Issues devolved to the Scottish Parliament include:

- Health
- Education and training
- Local government
- Social work
- Housing
- Planning
- Tourism, including financial assistance to the tourist industry
- Law and home affairs, including the court system
- The police and fire services
- The environment
- Natural and built heritage
- Sport and the arts
- Agriculture, forestry and fishing
- Some aspects of transport, including the Scottish road network, ports and harbours

Source: Michael Moran, *Politics and Governance in the UK*, Palgrave, 2005.

The committee system

Within the Scottish Parliament a committee system has been established, shadowing the policy areas mentioned above, in order to oversee and scrutinise policy development (see Box 5.2). Apart from their roles as scrutinisers of parliamentary business, the committees are also designed to take evidence from professional bodies and to process public petitions on matters of general importance. These committees are cross-party and are assembled to reflect party balance within the parliament. A committee has between five and fifteen Members of the Scottish Parliament (**MSPs**) as members. Membership of committees is proposed by the **Parliamentary Bureau**, the body responsible for liaising with the political-parties to ensure that the functions of parliament run smoothly. After discussions are led by the Parliamentary Bureau, the whole parliament approves suggestions as to which MSPs are to be members of a committee. MSPs who are not members of a committee can take part in its public proceedings but cannot vote.

Each committee then has a convener whose job it is to chair the sessions and determine the agenda. The members of the committee must choose a convener from a particular political party decided by parliament. In addition, each committee normally has a deputy convener who will chair meetings in the convener's absence. All of the conveners in the Scottish Parliament meet on a regular basis to discuss the progress and management of committees. This group is known as the **Conveners' Group**.

Since the advent of devolution, the committee system has proved to be vital to the workings of the parliament, and committee members have an extensive and often exhausting workload. One of the drawbacks of the committee system, however, is the limited number of MSPs available to sit on the committees. Members of the **Scottish Executive** cannot sit on committees, neither can the leaders of the Conservative and SNP oppositions nor the parliament's presiding officer and his deputy. This severely curtails the number of MSPs who are free to make up the relevant committees, a problem mirrored in the Welsh Assembly. Hence, some MSPs have to sit on more than one committee thus doubling their workload. While certain commentators and critics would say that this ensures the Scottish public is

---

**Box 5.2 Mandatory(M) and subject(S) committees of the
Scottish Parliament**

- Audit (M)
- Communities (S)
- Education (S)
- Enterprise and Culture (S)
- Environment and Rural Development (S)
- Equal Opportunities (M)
- European and External Relations (M)
- Finance (M)
- Health (S)
- Justice 1 (S)
- Justice 2 (S)
- Local Government and Transport (S)
- Procedures (M)
- Public Petitions (M)
- Standards and Public Appointments (M)
- Subordinate Legislation (M)
- Private Bills

Sources: Henig, Stanley, *Modernising Britain*, Kogan Page, 2002 and
www.scottish.parliament.uk

---

getting 'value for money' from their elected representatives, in terms
of the actual quality of service and delivery, this overloading is hardly
an ideal situation.

The passage of bills

Bills are normally introduced by the Scottish Executive, as they tend
to derive from policy proposals which have featured in the manifestos
of the political parties that have succeeded in gaining power; in the
case of the present executive, the Labour and Liberal Democrat
parties. These bills are known as 'executive bills'. However, bills can
also originate from sources such as the parliamentary committees –
these are termed 'committee bills' – and individual MSPs. The latter
are labelled 'members' bills'. Nevertheless, regardless of where the

bill stems from, the process for transforming it into an act remains the same. This is because, whenever a bill is introduced to the Scottish Parliament, it has to pass through three stages before it becomes law.

Stage 1 This is where consideration of the general principles of the bill – its aims and objectives – is dealt with by the parliamentary committee that has been designated to deal with this particular piece of legislation. After scrutinising the detail, the committee will report its findings to the parliament and, if parliament agrees to the bill's general principles, it will then be referred back to the committee for the next stage of the process to take place.

Stage 2 At this stage a more detailed consideration of the bill is undertaken. This will include contemplating any amendments to the bill that have been proposed by the Scottish Executive and by opposition MSPs.

Stage 3 This is the final consideration of the bill, in its amended form, by the entire parliament who will then vote on whether the bill should be passed or rejected.

After a bill is passed, having successfully completed all three stages of the process, it is then submitted for Royal Assent. It is only when Royal Assent is granted that the bill goes on the Statute Book as Act of the Scottish Parliament.

The Scottish Parliament and the issue of tax

Having observed the devolved powers and committee structure operating within the Scottish Parliament, certain similarities with other models of devolution in the United Kingdom, and elsewhere, become apparent. One area in which the Scottish Parliament is very distinctive, however, from its Welsh cousin, for instance, is in its ability to raise or lower the basic rates of income tax and business rates in Scotland. The main funding for the Scottish Parliament, at present, comes from a block grant from the British Exchequer. This transaction is similar to the past '**block grant**' system of payment that saw a set amount of money transferring from Whitehall to Scotland for the purpose of public expenditure. Nevertheless, the

Scottish Parliament has had the authority, since its inception, to vary the level of income tax, up or down, by 3 pence in every £1. This is what is known as the parliament's 'tax-varying' powers. Though opponents and critics of devolution sometimes mischievously dub this procedure the 'tartan tax', this devolved fiscal power enables Scotland to be more adaptable in its economic planning. This is because the Scottish Executive knows that, if needed, additional funds could be raised without having to make an appeal to the Treasury in Whitehall. Despite having this devolved power at its disposal, any serious discussion about raising or lowering tax rates has yet to emerge from within the Scottish Executive or the Scottish Parliament as a whole.

Tensions and disagreements

Under the terms of the Scotland Act (1998), the only way in which the Secretary of State for Scotland can interfere into the workings and decision-making of the Scottish Parliament is if he/she believes that a bill going through the Scottish Parliament contravenes, or is incompatible with, international laws or agreements. In that instance, the Secretary of State could veto the will of the Scottish Parliament or Scottish Executive. Furthermore, under Section 28 (7) of the Scotland Act, Westminster could, under certain circumstances, impose legislation on Scotland. If any of these scenarios were to occur, it would inevitably heighten tensions between the administration in Edinburgh and the British government in London. For example, the vetoing of any Scottish legislation by a secretary of state, who is a member of the British cabinet, would undoubtedly be perceived in many quarters in Scotland as a 'Britain first, Scotland second' decision. Similarly, should governments of different political shades be in charge in Scotland and Westminster then clashes over policy direction or political philosophy could ensue. Neither of these has yet to happen and therefore any consequences from such an action are purely speculation at this time. If either of the above were to happen, however, it could lead, in the short term, to the first real political crisis that devolution has thrown up. Alternatively, it could, in the long term, lead to a hardening of the 'independence' line that is held by some people within Scotland.

Building a new institution

The location for the Scottish Parliament is Edinburgh, Scotland's ancient capital. The parliament initially met in the Church of Scotland Assembly Hall on The Mound. It was soon felt, however, that this meeting place was inadequate, and therefore an innovative building should be created to symbolise the new political climate in Scotland. Enric Miralles, the Catalan architect, was commissioned to design the new parliament building. A site was identified opposite Holyrood Palace, at the bottom of the Royal Mile in Edinburgh, and construction work began. Before long, however, the excitement about this fresh political and public space dampened as the spiralling cost of the building became headline news, predominantly within the Scottish media but also further afield. Moreover, arguments about the cost and the time-scale of the building work were used by opponents of the devolution settlement to vindicate their view that devolution would turn out to be an expensive, and overambitious, bureaucratic project. Whichever side of the debate people choose to support, there is little doubt that the outcome, though still controversial, is a state-of-the-art parliament building that has succeeded in picking up several awards for its architectural design. The new parliament, often referred to as 'Holyrood', was formally opened by the Queen on 9 October 2004.

The Scottish Executive

The Scottish Executive is, in effect, the government of Scotland. Its role in the day-to-day governance of Scotland is similar to the Cabinet's role at Westminster. In the financial year 2005–6 it managed a budget of more than £27 billion. This figure is due to rise to over £30 billion in 2007–8.

When the Scottish Executive was set up, the powers of the Scottish Office were transferred to it. So, for instance, the civil servants who worked for the Scottish Office automatically began working for a new master in the guise of the Scottish Executive. Furthermore, all the links and partnerships that the old Scottish Office had nurtured were transmitted to the Scottish Executive. As a consequence, the Scottish Executive started to operate in a climate in which the complex interaction between the governing political party and a reputable bureaucracy, a widespread **quango** system, and the various groups within civil society, was already well established. Furthermore, pressure groups have played an important role in this process (see Box 5.3 below).

Box 5.3 Pressure groups and devolution in Scotland

- Pressure groups are non-party organisations, such as Scotland Against Nuclear Dumping, that attempt to shape and influence government policy to reflect their concerns.
- Pressure groups use a variety of activities, such as petitions, demonstrations, public meetings, etc. to influence policy-makers.
- Pressure groups have been active for many years in Scottish politics but they have had more opportunities to influence matters since devolution.
- As has been the case in Wales, the Scottish Parliament has seen increased activity among pressure groups and lobbying firms. This has meant that politicians cannot simply ignore the arguments of pressure groups, as they may have done before the advent of devolution.
- *Shaping Scotland's Parliament*, the report of the Consultative Steering Group, produced in 1999, encouraged consultation and the sharing of power among the people of Scotland, the legislators and the Scottish Executive. Pressure-group activity was therefore given a green light.
- Furthermore, First Minister Jack McConnell has stated that he is keen to see pressure groups applying pressure on politicians in the Scottish Parliament, as he argues that they represent civil society and the democratic process in Scotland. New Labour also sees the recognition of pressure-group activity as an acknowledgement that Scottish society is democratic and socially inclusive.
- ASH Scotland, the anti-smoking organisation, is one of the pressure groups that has succeeded in getting official recognition from the Scottish Executive as it has helped produce joint policy documents on tobacco with NHS Health Scotland.

Source: D. Watts, 'Pressure Group activity in Post-Devolution Scotland' in *Talking Politics* (January 2006), pp. 16–19.

The relationship between ministers – the elected politicians – and civil servants within the Scottish Executive is so interwoven that, within the Scottish political scene, both are referred to as 'the Executive'. While this joint labelling can help to present to the electorate a picture of unity, it can also be detrimental in that the faults of one sector are transferred to the other. Use of the terms 'government' and 'civil service' would make life so much easier for the people of Scotland.

As for the political make-up of the Scottish Executive, Box 5.4 (below) shows how the votes of the last Scottish Parliament Election, in 2003, led to the continuation of the Labour-Liberal Democrat coalition that had ruled since 1999, following the first elections to the Scottish Parliament. Coalition government demands that a policy programme is agreed upon from the outset. That is why, upon taking office in 2003, the Scottish Executive laid out its plans and priorities in a fifty-one-page programme entitled the 'Partnership Agreement'.

Box 5.4 Elections for the Scottish Parliament, May 2003 (1999 in brackets)

Party	Constituency votes %	Constituency seats	Regional list votes %	Regional list seats	Total seats
Labour	34.6 (38.8)	46 (53)	29.3 (33.6)	4 (3)	50 (56)
SNP	23.9 (28.7)	9 (7)	20.9 (27.3)	18 (28)	27 (35)
Cons	16.6 (15.5)	3 (0)	15.5 (15.4)	15 (18)	18 (18)
Lib Dem	15.4 (14.2)	13 (12)	11.8 (12.4)	4 (5)	17 (17)
Greens	0 (0)	0 (0)	6.9 (3.6)	7 (1)	7 (1)
Scottish Socialist	6.2 (1.0)	0 (0)	6.7 (2.0)	6 (1)	6 (1)
Others	3.4	2	9.0	2	4 (1)

Source: Robert Leach et al., *British Politics*, Palgrave, 2006.

How Scotland votes

The system for electing members to the Scottish Parliament is a form of proportional representation known as the **additional member system** (AMS). The idea of AMS and, indeed, any system of proportional representation, is to try to make everybody's vote count, in a democratic sense. The intention of AMS, therefore, is to ensure that the share of seats that each party receives reflects, as closely as possible, its level of support among voters. Consequently, there should not be any 'wasted' votes. The Scottish system also allows each constituency contested at the time of the Scottish Parliament elections – which incidentally mirror the constituencies used for Westminster elections – to have its own representative; its constituency MSP.

When it comes to the day of the election, each eligible voter at an election for the Scottish Parliament has two voters. The first vote cast is for the constituency vote, whereupon the candidate who gains the largest number of votes becomes that constituency's MSP; this is the 'first-past-the-post' system. There is a total of seventy-three constituencies.

The second vote that the public has is a list vote. Here, political parties provide lists of nominations for election on a regional basis. A region is larger than a constituency. Indeed, a region consists of a cluster of constituencies. There are eight regions at present. Each of the regions has seven seats in the Scottish Parliament, making a total of fifty-six seats. Members elected to these AMS seats are known within the Scottish political system as 'regional members'. The regions chosen for the Scottish Parliament elections are the same as those used in the European Parliament elections. Those regions are:

- Highlands and Islands
- North-east Scotland
- Mid Scotland and Fife
- West of Scotland
- Glasgow
- Central Scotland
- Lothians
- South of Scotland

Every Scottish resident is represented by one constituency MSP and seven regional MSPs. So the Scottish Parliament differs from the British parliament where only one elected member represents the local area. In Scotland, every member of the electorate has a total of eight MSPs who represent them in the Scottish Parliament. If the numbers of constituency and regional members are added together, they comprise the 129 members of the Scottish Parliament. Irrespective of how they are elected, however, once inside the parliament, each MSP has the same rights and responsibilities.

Membership of the Scottish Executive

As noted earlier, the Scottish Executive is currently a coalition executive. This has come about because Labour, the largest party in terms of the number of seats it holds at Holyrood, is unable to rule alone as it has not got an overall majority in parliament. The Scottish Labour Party has therefore entered into a governing coalition with the Liberal Democrats. Box 5.5 (opposite) shows the present make-up of the Scottish Executive. The party denomination of the individuals is shown alongside. The clearest example of this shared duty and responsibility is evident in the two foremost office-holders. As a result, it can be seen that Jack McConnell, First Minister since 2001, is the Labour MSP for Motherwell and Wishaw while his Deputy, Nicol Stephen, is the Liberal Democrat MSP for Aberdeen South and the leader of the Scottish Liberal Democrats. Between them, Jack McConnell and Nicol Stephen are responsible for, and in overall charge of, the development, implementation and presentation of Scottish Executive policies.

After a Scottish parliamentary election is held – once every four years – a first minister is formally nominated by the parliament. If acceptable, that person is then appointed by the Queen, in her capacity as head of state. The duty of the first minister is then to appoint a cabinet (the executive) who must have been agreed upon by parliament, and who must meet with the approval of the Queen. Box 5.6 (page 78) shows the duties of the First Minister for Scotland and the Secretary of State for Scotland.

To be a member of the Scottish Executive you have to have been elected, in the first instance, as a Member of the Scottish Parliament

Box 5.5 The Scottish Executive, 2006

First Minister	Jack McConnell (L)
Deputy First Minister and Minister for Enterprise and Lifelong Learning	Nicol Stephen (LD)
Deputy Minister for Enterprise and Lifelong Learning	Allan Wilson (L)
Minister for Justice	Cathy Jamieson (L)
Deputy Minister for Justice	Hugh Henry (L)
Minister for Health and Community Care	Andy Kerr (L)
Deputy Minister for Health and Community Care	Lewis Macdonald (L)
Minister for Education and Young People	Peter Peacock (L)
Deputy Minister for Education and Young People	Robert Brown (LD)
Minister for Finance and Public Service Reform	Tom McCabe (L)
Deputy Minister for Finance and Parliamentary Business	George Lyon (LD)
Minister for Environment and Rural Development	Ross Finnie (LD)
Deputy Minister for Environment and Rural Development	Rhona Brankin (L)
Minister for Communities	Malcolm Chisholm (L)
Deputy Minister for Communities	Johann Lamont (L)
Minister for Parliamentary Business	Margaret Curran (L)
Minister for Tourism, Culture and Sport	Patricia Ferguson (L)
Minister for Transport	Tavish Scott (LD)
Lord Advocate	Colin Boyd, QC
Solicitor General	Elish Angiolini, QC

(L) = Labour, (LD) = Liberal Democrat

Source: Scottish Parliament website.

(MSP). The only exceptions to this rule are the Lord Advocate and the Solicitor General whose tasks include overseeing the Crown Office and the Procurator Fiscal Service and offering legal advice to Scottish ministers. In the everyday language of Scottish politics and society, the members of the Scottish Executive tend to be referred to as 'the Scottish ministers'.

Box 5.6 Duties of the First Minister and the Secretary of State for Scotland

First Minister:

- Heads the Scottish Executive
- Oversees his/her party's programme for government
- Nominates ministers to serve in the Scottish Executive
- Leader of his/her party in the Scottish Parliament
- Takes Questions in Parliament
- Liaises with secretary of state on policy matters
- Represents the parliament and executive at official functions
- Keeper of Her Majesty's Seal (appointed by the Treaty of Union)

Secretary of State for Scotland

- Guardian of the Scotland Act and therefore responsible for the smooth running of devolution
- Liaises with the First Minister and the Scottish Executive
- Represents Scotland's interests at the British parliament and cabinet
- Shares duties with First Minister for representing Scotland in discussions and meetings with overseas delegations
- Current incumbent, Douglas Alexander, combines the role of Secretary of State for Scotland with his post as Secretary of State for Transport in the British parliament

The Scottish Parliament and Europe

For many years, there has been an underlying assumption among some political observers that a Scottish parliament would be far more pro-European in its outlook than any government based at Westminster. While this pro-Europeanism has been overexaggerated, the historical links between Scotland and France – 'the Auld Alliance' – have been used as a basis for Scotland's future relationship with countries on the European mainland. Before the 1997 referendum, one of the arguments put forward by those in favour of devolution was that a Scottish parliament could leapfrog London in order to provide the people of Scotland with a direct 'voice in Europe'.

The reality of a 'voice in Europe' is somewhat different, however. This is because the Scottish Parliament's relationship with the European Union is complicated for several reasons. In the Scotland Act (1998), discussions about macro-EU legislation, and direct dealings with the European Union, were among the reserved powers that Westminster refused to devolve. It is believed by those in Westminster that the role of Scottish ministers should be one of supporting the British line in whatever negotiations are taking place. Nevertheless, Scottish ministers can, through invitation, attend meetings of the Council of the European Union. Ultimately, however, even if members of the Scottish Executive are present during discussions, it is the British minister, responsible to the prime minister and the British cabinet, who retains overall responsibility for any negotiations that are held. So, engaging in direct dialogue and voting on EU issues, along 'nation-state' lines, remains the preserve of the British government and its ministers.

Nevertheless, despite this apparent rebuff to the new institution in Edinburgh, the Scottish Parliament, as well as seeking to find the best way to implement EU initiatives within Scotland, takes seriously its commitment to forging relationships with the regional governments in Europe, such as the Lander in Germany. These links with political institutions throughout Europe, and especially those within what is sometimes labelled 'the new Europe' – the newly emerging political and economic regions – are seen as important for the Scottish Parliament as they can aid in promoting '**horizontal partnerships**' between the 'nation-region' of Scotland and similar 'nation-regions' such as Catalonia or Brittany. Further, the Scottish Parliament has also been active in its attempts to persuade the business community within Europe to consider investing in the Scottish economy. Part of this exercise involves promoting Scotland as an ideal place in which to live and work.

To facilitate these and other matters, the Scottish Parliament has a mandatory European Committee with a membership of thirteen MSPs. This committee has to interpret, and then act upon, European Union legislation which relates to Scotland, such as monitoring the use of the European Structural Fund programme. To these ends, it is vitally important that all members of the Scottish Parliament are fully aware of legislative developments that emanate from the European Union. The European Committee of the Scottish Parliament also has to ensure that the policies and laws stemming from the Scottish Executive are in tune with EU legislation and practice. Thus, the precise remit of the European Committee, according to Rule 6.8 of the Standing Orders of the Scottish Parliament, demands that the committee is to consider and report on:

- proposals for European Communities legislation;
- the implementation of European Communities legislation;
- any European Communities or European Union issue.

On 5 March 2003 the Scottish Parliament extended the remit of the committee to cover the following additional issues:

- the development and implementation of the Scottish administration's links with countries and territories outside Scotland, the European Communities (and their institutions) and other international organisations;
- co-ordination of the international activities of the Scottish administration.

Upon taking charge of these extra tasks, the committee's name was altered from the European Committee to the European and External Relations Committee.

Most of the discussions and analysis concerning EU and Scottish legislative and policy matters can be comfortably addressed by the European and External Relations Committee. Some of the more complicated issues of policy and law, however, which may require negotiations at an EU-national government level, have to be referred to the suitable government department at a British level. It is important to remember in all this, therefore, that, even though the Scottish Parliament is a relatively powerful political institution with primary legislative powers, any act of the Scottish Parliament cannot become law if it is incompatible with European Union law. This stipulation is enshrined under Section 29 (2) of the Scotland Act (1998).

Parliamentary business

Box 5.7 gives an example of a day's political business at the Scottish Parliament. Like many parliamentary institutions, the business of committees usually takes place in the morning while plenary submis-

Box 5.7 Scottish Parliament Business Programme (example)

Thursday, 25 May 2006

9.15 a.m. **Parliamentary Bureau** Motions
followed by Stage 3 Proceedings: Police, Public Order and Criminal Justice (Scotland) Bill.

11.40 a.m. General Question Time

12 noon First Minister's Question Time

2.15 p.m. Themed Question Time
Enterprise, Transport and Lifelong Learning
Justice and Law Officers

2.55 p.m. Continuation of Stage 3 Proceedings: Police, Public Order and Criminal Justice (Scotland) Bill
followed by Parliamentary Bureau Motions

5.00 p.m. Decision Time
followed by Members' Business – Debate on the subject of S2M-3983 Trish Goodman: The Trafficking of Impoverished Women into Forced Prostitution in Scotland.

Source: Scottish Parliament website.

sions tend to begin around midday. Plenary sessions are chaired by the Presiding Officer (the Speaker), whose task it also is to regulate the day-to-day business of the parliament. For the record, some of the other tasks undertaking by the Presiding Officer include administering oaths of allegiance in the parliament (held after MSPs have been elected), submitting bills for their Royal Assent, and chairing the **Scottish Parliamentary Corporate Body** (SPCB), that is responsible for staffing, overseeing the updating of facilities, and so forth. Throughout the day in the parliament building, ministers and individual MSPs will also have meetings among themselves as well as with outside organisations or individuals. These take place in committee rooms outside the debating chamber.

Sewell motions

As the Scottish Parliament has established itself, the use of 'Sewell motions' has grown. In the first five years of the parliament, more than fifty Sewell motions were passed. Sewell motions comprise a mechanism whereby the British parliament can legislate on Scotland's behalf. The Scottish Executive can then add the act to its own legislative programme. While the Labour Party argues that Sewell motions are beneficial, as they can speed up the legislative process, the opposition, and most notably the SNP, contend that Sewell motions do not allow the Scottish Parliament any effective means to amend or oppose changes made to a bill that derives from Westminster. For the SNP, therefore, this undermines the Scottish Parliament, and the devolutionary process. The current debate in Scotland regarding this contentious issue tends to centre on whether the granting of Sewell motions facilitates unproblematical governance in Scotland, or whether Sewell motions are merely a tool through which centralised rule from Westminster continues to be enacted. Whichever view one adopts, the continued, and increasing, use of Sewell motions undoubtedly holds back the reins of those who see devolution as a smooth and rapid stepping stone to independence.

Sub-national Scotland: local government

In the 1970s many people working within local government in Scotland had serious concerns about the arrival of devolution. This was because they envisaged their limited political autonomy being eroded more quickly under a Scottish parliament than it seemed to be wearing away under the British government. Scottish local government had undergone a major reorganisation in the mid-1970s, and many involved in local politics in Scotland just wanted to see a period of stability and consolidation rather than any further changes and upheavals. By the 1980s and 1990s, however, local government officials and representatives had climbed on board the devolution train, thanks in part to the intense involvement of the **Convention of Scottish Local Authorities** (CoSLA) with pro-devolution organisations, such as the Scottish Constitutional Convention. Furthermore, by 1995, the Conservative Party had lost control of its

Box 5.8 Scottish local government functions (since devolution)

Local government has a variety of roles and functions. These can be summarised under four main headings:

1. **Provision of Services** Local authorities have responsibility for the planning, resourcing and direct provision of services that are within the competence of the Scottish Parliament. To help provide these services, local government works increasingly in partnership with the private and voluntary sectors as well as with executive agencies such as Communities Scotland.
2. **Strategic planning** Local authorities provide a strategic planning framework, setting objectives for their area over the long term.
3. **Regulation** Local authorities have regulatory functions, such as the granting of certain licences, and registration and inspection functions.
4. **Community leadership** The Local Government Act 2003 has added this role by placing local government as the key agency in the community-planning process and providing local authorities with a 'power of well-being'.

Source: Scottish Parliament website.

remaining local councils and, with it, the last stems of opposition to devolution just fizzled out.

In 2003 the Local Government in Scotland Act was introduced. This is seen as being key to the Scottish Executive's desire to introduce reforms and oversee the 'modernisation' of local government north of the border. The measures in the act have been framed in such as way that they promote partnerships with other bodies and with the community, and are designed to put the quality of services, and their delivery, at the forefront of the local authorities' commitment to the public. At the heart of this is the concept known as '**Best value**', with its ethos of continuous improvement across all aspects of local authority functions.

As the 2003 act embodies a commitment to consult the public, many observers have seen this as a further decentralisation of power within Scotland; albeit that the role of the general public is naturally somewhat limited in the actual policy-making process. Nevertheless, 'communities', be they defined by their geography or their shared interests, such as is the case with the elderly community, must now be seen to be active partners who engage in constructive dialogue with local government and with the Scottish Parliament in order to formulate policies that are deemed to be democratic, inclusive, and to the benefit of the many and not just the few. Prior to the 2003 act, the Scottish Executive had pre-empted the role of communities by establishing '**Communities Scotland**' as an agency to promote community regeneration.

The role of the quangos

As elsewhere in Britain the roles of the quasi-autonomous non-governmental organisations, or quangos, expanded rapidly in the years preceding devolution. In Scotland, the quangos are sometimes given the alternative title NDPBs, or non-departmental public bodies. The key period for quango expansionism was the 1980s and early 1990s, when prime ministers Margaret Thatcher and John Major sought to diminish the powers of local authorities – often Labour-led – which challenged the prevailing political orthodoxies. By 1995, 160 quangos were operating under the auspices of the Scottish Office. By packing the quangos with business people and professionals who were sympathetic to the Conservative government's aims and objectives, the Conservatives felt that they could secure a comfortable passage for their public-service reforms. Along these lines, therefore, private-sector principles were widely introduced into public-sector departments and agencies. This 'politicisation' of the quangos infuriated organisations such as the Scottish Constitutional Convention which campaigned for the democratisation of the quango system.

Since devolution, the Scottish quangos have come under far greater scrutiny from a Scottish Parliament that rightly sees itself as the guardian of the public purse. Interestingly, though, direct responsibility for the quangos, stemming from the Scotland Act, is the preserve of the Scottish Executive rather than the Scottish Parliament. In 2000 the then Finance Minister, Jack McConnell, produced a paper that led to consultations about having more transparency when it came to appointments to quangos in Scotland. In 2001 the Scottish Executive decided to review the 'Quango state' and they recommended the abolition of fifty-two of the then 180 NDPBs in operation. While some were to be scrapped altogether, it was suggested that others could be merged. Hence, when it comes to the quangos, there has been a noticeable change of direction in Scottish political thinking and, recently, a cautious and protective position has been taken by the Scottish Parliament to the work of the quangos, forty of which have disappeared since the Scottish Executive's review.

....

✔ What you should have learnt from reading this chapter

- Some aspects of Scottish civic and political life remained relatively unchanged after the 1707 Act of Union.
- The Scottish Parliament possesses primary law-making powers.
- The power of the quangos in Scotland has been curbed since the advent of devolution.
- Elections to the Scottish Parliament use a different voting system from that used during elections to the British parliament.
- The Scottish Parliament has developed close working links with the European Union and with other parliaments and assemblies within Europe and beyond.

🔎 Glossary of key terms

Additional member system (AMS) The system of proportional representation used in elections to the Scottish Parliament.
Best value Seeks to promote a climate of continuous improvement within local government in order that local authorities can deliver improved services year after year.
Block grant Payment from the UK Exchequer to the Scottish and Welsh Offices to oversee public expenditure on those countries.
Communities Scotland An executive agency of the Scottish Executive. It was formed in November 2001 to promote community regeneration.
Conveners' group Seeks to promote and co-ordinate the work of the parliamentary committees. The group meets on a weekly basis.
CoSLA The Convention of Scottish Local Authorities. CoSLA is the representative voice of Scotland's unitary local authorities.
Horizontal partnerships These occur whenever the Scottish Parliament attempts to create links and a working relationship with a similar institution, normally within Europe, whose composition, range of legislative powers and general geographical, historical or political position equates with that which can found within the Scottish experience.

MSP Member of the Scottish Parliament. The title given to the democratically elected members of the Scottish Parliament.

Parliamentary Bureau A cross-party forum that prepares the daily order of business for parliament. It also proposes the membership and remit of parliamentary committees.

Primary legislation The ability to draw up, and subsequently pass, new laws within the confines of the Scottish Parliament. Primary legislation enables the Scottish Executive to do this without having to seek permission from any outside body.

Quangos Quasi-autonomous non-governmental organisations. These are semi-independent administrative bodies that have traditionally controlled certain areas of public policy and expenditure.

Scottish Executive In effect, the 'Scottish Cabinet'. This is the body that holds ultimate political power within the Scottish Parliament.

Scottish Parliament The actual institution of government in Scotland. Usually identified as being the parliament building itself, though it does include the entire machinery of government in Scotland including the elected personnel.

Scottish Parliamentary Corporate Body (SPCB) The body responsible for overseeing staffing and estates in the Scottish Parliament. The SPCB is made up of four MSPs plus the Presiding Officer of the Parliament.

? Likely examination questions

Discuss the ways in which the Scottish Parliament is able to make primary legislation.

How has devolution affected Scotland's relationship with the European Union?

Detail the ways in which local government in Scotland has changed since the arrival of devolution.

In what ways could the committee system of the Scottish Parliament be improved?

Helpful websites

www.scottish.parliament.uk The Scottish Parliament website. (Information on the Scottish Executive can also be accessed on the same website.)

www.cosla.gov.uk Further information on local government in Scotland can be found on both the CoSLA website.

www.audit-scotland.gov.uk The Audit Scotland website.

Suggestions for further reading

P. Lynch, *Scottish Government and Politics*, Edinburgh University Press, 2001.

J. Mitchell, *Governing Scotland*, Palgrave, 2003.

P. Schlesinger et al., *Open Scotland?* Edinburgh University Press, 2001.

A. Trench (ed.), *The Dynamics of Devolution*, Imprint Academic, 2005.

CHAPTER 6

Political Parties and Politics in Scotland

Contents

Overview

As was noted in chapter 5, the political scene in Scotland has been transformed since the arrival of devolution. Barring any major political upheaval, it is expected that it will continue to change, in an evolutionary manner, as devolved government embeds itself and political parties have to find ways to react to political scenarios that have never before been encountered. In this chapter the political parties which have established a foothold in the Scottish Parliament will be analysed. Some of these parties, such as Labour and the Conservatives, will be familiar to students of politics, while others, such as the Scottish Socialist Party and the Scottish Senior Citizens Unity Party, are more recent additions to the list of political parties that have attained some parliamentary representation.

Key issues to be covered in this chapter

- The unique nature of Scottish politics
- The four major political parties in Scotland
- The rise of the Scottish Socialist Party
- The Greens and devolution
- Senior citizens and devolutionary politics
- Scottish political parties: the future

The unique nature of Scottish politics

It can be claimed that every political system, anywhere in the world, has its own unique characteristics. As mentioned previously, Scotland has its own cultural and political history that identifies it as a separate nation; albeit that its history and its politics overlap and interweave with those of its neighbours and form part of what is termed 'British history' and 'British politics'. So Scottish identity – political and otherwise – can sit comfortably in what some commentators have described as being the '**Four Nations**' model of Britain. As this book is attempting to do, however, the difference between these nations has to be acknowledged and assessed. It could be argued that the Scottish party political system, pre-devolution, looked similar to the Westminster model. Conversely, post-devolution, the Scottish political landscape appears markedly different as smaller parties and coalition government are now an integral part of the Scottish parliamentary scene. These political changes, added to Scotland's distinct culture and heritage, have meant that the structure of Scottish society has become even more distinctive in recent years.

Scottish Labour Party

While the Labour Party has long played a significant part in Scottish politics, it has never quite attained the hegemonic position in Scotland that it enjoys in Wales. It has maintained a solid level of support, however, especially in the industrial belt of Central Scotland. There has also been widespread backing across Scotland for the party's traditional concerns about achieving social justice through the implementation of a comprehensive welfare-state system. Thus, despite attempts by some politicians to reduce it across Britain as a whole, a sense of '**political collectivism**' is still in evidence across Scotland.

When it came to the issue of devolution, it would be fair to comment that many people within Scottish Labour in the 1970s were unenthusiastic about the idea of decentralised rule. This was because, at that time, most Labour Party supporters still saw the future in terms of centralisation, wherein industries could be nationalised and run by the state, the state machinery being centred in London. By the 1980s, however, opinion within the Scottish Labour

Party was changing, and many party members started to see devolution as the means through which the effects of Thatcherism could firstly be challenged and then, ultimately, reversed. Thus, devolution was seen by some within the Scottish Labour Party as a way of preserving, and developing, the welfare-state system that had been built upon in Britain since 1945. This view was further reinforced after the 1987 General Election when Labour picked up a majority of seats in Scotland but was frustrated by the return of the Conservative Party at Westminster because of the support given to the Conservatives by the English electorate.

Despite a clear string of successes in elections, such as in the 1987 General Election mentioned above, it has become evident, at least in the last couple of decades, that Labour's position as the leading and, since 1997, the governing party in Scotland has been challenged by the SNP. As the Scottish National Party repositioned itself as a 'centre-left' political force, so Labour was faced with contending with a party that could appeal to social democrats and socialists while, at the same time, playing the patriotic card. Labour's answer to the SNP threat was to re-emphasise its commitment to Scotland as a separate social, political and cultural unit; in effect, the party had to become one of '**pragmatic nationalists**'. The Scottish Labour Party hoped that this portrayal of the party as 'pragmatic nationalists' would persuade those people who could be described as 'soft nationalists' to stick with Labour rather than pledge their allegiance to the Scottish Nationalists. It appears to have done this quite successfully as its record in office, since the advent of devolution, demonstrates.

The Scottish Labour Party since devolution

The Scottish Labour Party gained the most votes of any party in the inaugural Scottish Parliament Election in 1999, and picked up fifty-six seats (fifty-three in the constituencies and three on the regional list). On 17 May, the Labour leader, Donald Dewar, became Scotland's First Minister. Dewar and Scottish Labour could not rule alone and therefore a coalition government was negotiated between Labour and the Liberal Democrats. As part of the deal, Jim Wallace, leader of the Scottish Liberal Democrats, became Deputy First Minister.

After Donald Dewar's premature death, on 11 October 2000, the party struggled to some extent to reassert itself. The new first minister, the MSP for Fife Central, Henry McLeish, defeated Jack McConnell in a ballot for the post. McLeish did not last very long in the job, however, as he resigned in November 2001 amid a scandal, known as the 'Officegate Scandal', involving allegations that he failed to register a business interest. He was succeeded in the position of first minister by the man he had defeated, Jack McConnell, who was unopposed.

The Scottish Labour Party has not been able to implement fully its own agenda in office because it has had to compromise with its coalition partner, the Liberal Democrats. Despite being the major party in Scotland – in terms of votes at the Scottish Parliament and general elections of recent years – the Scottish Labour Party has had some difficulty in agenda setting. Though Scottish Labour has attempted, and probably succeeded, in presenting itself in a different light from **New Labour** at Westminster, it could be argued, nevertheless, that it is still too early to judge how considerable the party's distinctly 'Scottish' approach has actually been.

Box 6.1 Jack McConnell: First Minister of the Scottish Parliament

- Born 30 June 1960
- Mathematics teacher
- Leader of Stirling District Council from 1990 to 1992
- Became General Secretary of the Scottish Labour Party in 1992
- Elected MSP for Motherwell and Wishaw in 1999
- Finance Minister in the initial Scottish Executive
- Defeated by Henry McLeish in the contest to find Donald Dewar's successor
- Education, Europe and External Affairs Minister under McLeish
- Became First Minister on 22 November 2001
- Acted swiftly upon taking office to rid the Scottish Executive of 'McLeish loyals'
- Dubbed 'Union Jack' by the SNP for his hostility towards the idea of Scottish independence

Scottish Liberal Democrats

The Scottish Liberal Democrats are the youngest of the 'big' political parties, having been established as late as 1988 following the merger of the Scottish Liberal Party and the Scottish Social Democratic Party (SDP). As was the case in the rest of the United Kingdom, Liberalism declined as an ideology in the early to mid-twentieth century. This meant that the Scottish Liberals lost seats that were once bastions of Liberalism and, in other instances, the Liberals failed to find enough candidates to fight seats at general elections. In 1955, for example, only five Liberal Party members contested seats in Scotland. Fascinatingly, the arrival of the SDP, in 1981, boosted '**centre ground**' political thinking in Scotland. Two years later, in the 1983 General Election, the Liberal-SDP Alliance managed to contest every available seat in Scotland. From that point, the Liberals, later to be the Liberal Democrats, have managed to offer a real centrist political alternative in Scotland.

Scottish Liberal Democrats: with devolution comes power!

The Scottish Liberal Democratic Party has always stressed its commitment to devolution by pointing out that it is a party that is itself devolved from the United Kingdom, or Federal, Liberal Democratic Party. On top of this, the Scottish Liberal Democrats also cite the long Liberal tradition of supporting a decentralised political culture in Britain. With the arrival of devolution, therefore, the Scottish Liberal Democrats felt confident and upbeat about the party's chances of shaping the path of devolved government in the years ahead.

The real impact for the Scottish Liberal Democrats came about, however, when it became apparent that the party would have to enter into coalition government with the Scottish Labour Party. For the Liberal Democrats, the notable success of this coalition, in its first term, was evidenced by the party's insistence that Labour drops its commitment to introduce up-front tuition fees for Scottish students studying at Scottish universities. In terms of overall political philosophy, the Scottish Liberal Democratic Party was trying to defend the idea of the universal welfare state at a time when it was under fire from those, including many within the Labour Party, who saw the free market, and the opening up of public-service provision to the private sector, as the solution to the difficulties encountered by some sectors of the welfare state. One example of the Scottish Liberal Democrats' determination to uphold, and actually increase, welfare provision came about with the party's insistence that the coalition government introduce free personal care for elderly people in Scotland.

The Scottish Liberal Democrats have continued to champion many of these themes during the second term of the Scottish Parliament, which has seen a continuation of the Labour/Liberal Democrat coalition. Battling away on the education front, it has been the Scottish Liberal Democrats who have pressed their Labour partners to ensure that they refrained from introducing the new system of university 'top-up' fees that were proposed, and accepted, in England.

Scottish National Party (SNP)

The Scottish National Party (SNP) was formed in 1934 from the amalgamation of two existing nationalist groupings, the National Party of Scotland and the Scottish Party. Like Plaid Cymru in Wales, the SNP had limited impact in the first few decades of its existence, and it was seen more as a pressure group and sometimes a social club than as a potent political force. What the SNP did succeed in doing, however, even during times when its electoral base was small, was to highlight the possibility of alternative methods of government for Scotland rather than merely the Westminster model that was being advocated by, for example, the Conservative and Unionist Party.

The SNP had a moderately successful period – in terms of electoral triumphs and an expansion in membership numbers – during the 1960s and 1970s. Much of this success can be attributed to the party's 'It's Scotland's Oil' campaign that succeeded in touching a raw nerve with those Scots who felt that the discovery of oil and gas reserves in Scottish waters should, first and foremost, aid the Scottish economy, rather than being siphoned off to the Treasury in London to be used for general expenditure. After this period, the SNP began to see the Labour Party as its real political enemy – launching into a rhetorical campaign in which Labour was described as 'London Labour' – and, with Labour moving to the right, the SNP began to reposition itself and describe its policies as 'socialist' or 'social democratic'. Hence, the battle for the left-of-centre ground in Scottish politics, and the claim as to who had the true interests of the Scottish people at heart, were really under way.

Alex Salmond and the SNP's push for devolution

In 1990 Alex Salmond took the leadership of the SNP, picking up 486 votes from party delegates against Margaret Ewing's 186. Salmond led the SNP for a decade from 1990 to 2000, before returning to assume the reins again in 2004. His leadership proved vital to furthering the case for a new political settlement in Scotland. Salmond sought to induce what he termed 'social democracy with a Scottish face'. In doing so, he was taking on Labour on what many deemed as being Labour's political ground. This was an astute tactical move as it meant that the media in Scotland, and occasionally further afield, would home in on this ideological battle. While the media studied the nature of the policies, the SNP, with Salmond to the fore, could push the case for Scottish self-government.

The fundamentalist/gradualist debate

However it positions itself in left/right terms, there is an ongoing debate within the SNP as to the pace at which the party should seek to transform Scotland's constitutional status. This debate remains in progress because the SNP has always had its **'gradualist'** and **'fundamentalist'** wings. The 'gradualists' seek independence through a 'ladder system' that involves, initially, the type of devolved government presently to be seen at Holyrood. The gradualists then hanker for an incremental process – possibly taking many years – that would eventually lead to a referendum on independence. Alternatively, those supporting the 'fundamentalist' outlook within the SNP argue for what has been termed the **'big bang'** approach to achieving self-government. This 'big bang' position would see independence coming about very shortly after a victory for the SNP at the polls. Those adopting the 'fundamentalist' stance contend that independence is an urgent necessity. They therefore claim that Scotland cannot afford to waste its time going through an evolutionary process to independence.

Box 6.2 Gradualism versus fundamentalism

Gradualism

- Dominant faction within the SNP since 1970s
- Pro-devolution: seen as a 'step in the right direction'
- Evolutionary road to independence
- More willing to co-operate with other political parties and campaigning organisations

Fundamentalism

- Smaller but vocal faction within the SNP
- Unconvinced about the purpose of devolution
- Fast track to independence: the 'big bang' approach
- Sceptical about the desire for independence among other political parties and organisations

The SNP: devolution as a stepping stone to independence!

With its mission to deliver independence to the people of Scotland, it would be easy and simplistic to claim that devolution is a 'halfway house' for the SNP and for other advocates of an independent Scotland. But, as seen in the debate highlighted above, there are internal tensions and disagreements about the correct way to proceed. Nevertheless, the SNP performed reasonably well at the 1999 Scottish Parliament Election. The party achieved second place overall, with 29 per cent of the first vote and 27 per cent of the second vote. This ensured a total of thirty-five seats in the first parliament.

In the election campaign, the SNP portrayed the Scottish Labour Party as puppets of New Labour in London. The SNP thus asked the people to vote for a Scottish-based party rather than a London-based organisation. Simultaneously, Salmond attacked the Liberal Democrats who, according to the SNP, were just waiting to form a coalition with Labour. When the results showed Labour with the most seats and likely to form a partnership with the Liberal Democrats, some voices with the fundamentalist camp of the SNP were raised to claim that the SNP should have been far more nationalistic in its rallying cries to the Scottish people. These fundamentalists see independence for Scotland as an 'historical inevitability'. The role of the SNP, they argue, is to facilitate it by presenting a strong nationalist case for secession from the United Kingdom. The leadership of the SNP, however, and the majority of its supporters, appear content at this time to accept the devolution process and to work to achieve an SNP majority at Holyrood. For them, devolution may well be a stepping stone to independence but the river that they have to cross remains very wide.

Scottish Conservative Party

In the 1950s the Scottish Conservative Party was on the crest of a wave. So much so, in fact, that, in the 1955 General Election, the Tories gained over 50 per cent of the vote in Scotland. Interestingly, at that time, many Conservatives in Scotland were still using the title 'the Unionist Party', a title used by the party mostly from 1886 to 1921 but, in some instances, maintained until the 1980s. Given the debate on home rule that was beginning to emerge at that time, the use of the label 'the Unionist Party' showed that Conservatives who used it were clearly signalling their adherence to maintaining the political and constitutional status quo.

The Scottish Conservative Party's steady decline since the 1950s has been put down to many factors. It is evident, however, that the Conservatives' passion for Unionism, and its intransigent position regarding the maintenance of the political and constitutional set-up of the United Kingdom, combined with a denial of the growing sense of national identity among Scottish people, did not commend it to those rising numbers among the electorate who were demanding radical change.

The final nail in the coffin, however, appeared to arrive with the Conservative administration of Margaret Thatcher who, it was perceived by many north of the border, placed the interests of England before those of Scotland. With all this as a backdrop, the Scottish Conservative Party was always likely to face difficulties with the establishment of devolved government as the Tories, more than any other party, had to come to terms with a new structure that had widespread electoral support but which was the antithesis of the core beliefs held by most Scottish Conservatives.

Scottish Conservative Party: devolution and renewal

Faced with the moral and electoral difficulties outlined above, it can be argued that the Scottish Conservatives have done fairly well since the onset of devolution. One key moment for the Conservatives came in 1998 when, after some soul searching, the party became far more 'Scottish' in the sense that it was granted more autonomy from Conservative Central Office in London, and it began to develop more focused policies that took account of the changes that devolution was about to bring. How far these changes can account for any Conservative resurgence in Scotland – limited as it may be – is open to debate. Nevertheless, there is now a maturity about the Scottish Conservative Party that did not exist a decade or so ago.

In electoral terms the Scottish Conservatives have undoubtedly benefited from the system of proportional representation (PR) that was introduced at the time of devolution. The Tories knew that this would be advantageous as projections released at the time of the 1997 General Election indicated. According to these figures, the Conservatives, who did not pick up a single first-past-the-post (FPTP) seat at that election, would have had thirteen seats if a PR system had been in use. This was further indication, if needed, that, despite its general hostility towards the concept of devolution, the Scottish Conservative Party would be in a position to gain seats and relaunch itself after elections to the Scottish Parliament took place.

At present, the Scottish Conservative Party has seventeen MSPs sitting at Holyrood. The current leader of the Tories in the Scottish Parliament is Annabel Goldie, a regional-list MSP for the West of Scotland. The Scottish Conservatives remain very upbeat about any renaissance in its fortunes, and the party claims that it has increased its support base through the Conservative Future Scotland movement. Added to this, the party also reported an increased membership in university campuses across Scotland. Moreover, some activists, such as Councillor Charlie Gilbert, Chairman of the Scottish Conservative Councillors' Association, have called for devolution to go one step further in order that politics can be truly grass-roots. Gilbert wishes to see the Scottish Tories adopting a 'localist agenda' with an emphasis on community politics, and with people given greater powers to scrutinise the work and decision-making of their local authorities. This is a theme that has its roots in earlier Conservative thought, with major Tory figures, such as Quintin Hogg and Edward Heath, as far back as the 1960s advancing notions about the dispersal of political power throughout communities. Furthermore, what is interesting, as far as contemporary politics is concerned, is that this call to disperse power also reverberates among other political parties in Scotland, such as the Scottish Liberal Democrats and the Scottish Greens.

Scottish Socialist Party (SSP)

The Scottish Socialist Party (SSP) was formed in 1998. It arose out of the umbrella organisation, the Scottish Socialist Alliance, which was an alliance of left-wing organisations. Its principal founders were Alan McCombes and Tommy Sheridan (see Box 6.3). The Scottish Socialist Party ideology combines **democratic socialism** with a call for Scottish independence. The party is also a founding member of the organisation known as the European Anticapitalist Left, and it has an active youth wing called Scottish Socialist Youth. The SSP manages to get its ideological message across through its weekly newspaper, the *Scottish Socialist Voice*.

The SSP made its mark in the 1999 Scottish Parliament Election that saw Tommy Sheridan become the party's first MSP. This period also saw the SSP picking up new members as some people within the Labour Party and the SNP favoured the more left-wing, pro-independence message put out by the Scottish Socialists. The early days of the party did not go completely smoothly, however, as some internal disagreements arose. These were mainly concerned with the issue of independence. On this issue, certain members of the SSP thought that it was more important to promote the party's socialist ideas than pushing the case for self-government for Scotland. The majority of the membership disagreed with this stance and, therefore, Scottish independence remains a priority for the SSP.

Box 6.3 Who is Tommy Sheridan?

- Tommy Sheridan has been an MSP since 1999 and represents the region of Glasgow
- Sheridan was the Convener of the Scottish Socialist Party (SSP) from 2003 to 2004
- A charismatic leader and fine orator, Sheridan often appears right at the top of opinion polls that seek to find Scotland's most respected politician
- One explanation for this may well be the stance that Sheridan took against the poll tax in Scotland
- As a councillor on Glasgow City Council, Sheridan was imprisoned for his actions against the charge's imposition

The SSP: going from strength to strength

In the 2003 Scottish Parliament Election, the Scottish Socialist Party gained six MSPs from the regional list. This gave the party a huge boost in its campaign to achieve an independent socialist Scotland. Shortly after the 2003 election, the party gained the services of Lloyd Quinlan, a former MSP, from the SNP. Also, the party received support from George Galloway MP who has said that the Respect Coalition, of which he is a member, has no plans to challenge the SSP in Scotland. Some trade unionists also spoke of the SSP in favourable terms around this time. Notably, the Rail, Maritime and Transport Workers Union (RMT) announced that its branches were free to affiliate to the SSP should they so wish. During this period, therefore, and with its support base increasing, the newly elected MSPs began to make their mark in the Scottish Parliament. This benefited the party as a whole as some of the pressure to present the SSP's case was now taken off the shoulders of Tommy Sheridan who had been in the media spotlight ever since his election in 1999.

In November 2004 Tommy Sheridan, for personal reasons, decided to relinquish his position as SSP Convener. A ballot was held to find a replacement for him. Colin Fox and Alan McCombes competed. At an SSP conference in February 2005, Fox defeated McCombes by 252 votes to 154. With Colin Fox now at the helm, the

SSP remains a small but powerful bloc within the Scottish Parliament and within Scottish politics as a whole.

Scottish Green Party

The Scottish Green Party (*Partaidh Uaine na h-Alba* in Scottish Gaelic) became a separate political party from the Green Party of England and Wales in 1990. The Scottish Greens wanted this separation as it showed the party's commitment to decentralisation. Apart from decentralisation and **environmental** concerns, the Scottish Green Party, like the Scottish Socialist Party, likes to emphasise its commitment to establishing an independent Scotland. In international terms, the Scottish Green Party is a member of the Global Greens organisation, and, within Europe, it is a full member of the European Federation of Green Parties.

The Scottish Green Party received 3.6 per cent of list votes in the 1999 Scottish Parliament Election. This gave the Greens its first MSP, Robin Harper, in the Lothians region. With representation in parliament, the Scottish Greens' profile was raised and its youth wing, Scottish Young Greens, grew in strength. This enabled it launch itself into the 2003 Parliamentary Election with renewed vigour.

With seven MSPs at Holyrood, since 2003, the Scottish Green Party is currently the fifth largest party at the Scottish Parliament. Two of those MSPs, Shiona Baird and Robin Harper, have adopted the roles of Co-convenor of the Greens and parliamentary co-leaders. The parliamentary responsibilities of the party's MSPs are outlined in Box 6.4. In policy terms, the Scottish Green Party campaigns for, among other environmental and peace issues, a 'Zero Waste' strategy for Scotland, the rejection of genetically modified (GM) crops, and the adoption of fair trade policies across Scotland as a whole.

Scottish Senior Citizens Unity Party (SSCUP)

The Scottish Senior Citizens Unity Party (SSCUP) was formed in February 2003. Astonishingly, less than three months later they had a Member of the Scottish Parliament. That MSP is John Swinburne, one of the party's founders, who is a list MSP representing the region of Central Scotland. Apart from his MSP duties and responsibilities

---

Box 6.4 Parliamentary responsibilities of Scottish Green Party MSPs

- **Shiona Baird** (North-east Scotland) is Co-Convener of the Scottish Green Party. She speaks on enterprise and lifelong learning, energy and waste. She sits on the Enterprise, Lifelong Learning and Culture Committee.
- **Mark Ballard** (Lothians) speaks on finance and public services. He sits on the Finance Committee.
- **Chris Ballance** (South of Scotland) speaks on nuclear issues, peace, arts, culture and tourism and parliamentary business.
- **Robin Harper** (Lothians) is Co-Convener of the Scottish Green Party. He speaks on education, young people and sport, and sits on the parliament's Audit Committee.
- **Patrick Harvie** (Glasgow) speaks on justice, communities, Europe and constitutional affairs. He sits on the Communities Committee.
- **Mark Ruskell** (Mid-Scotland and Fife) speaks on the environment and fisheries. He is Co-Convener of the parliament's Environment and Rural Development Committee. He also leads the Green Campaign for a Food Revolution and GM Liability.
- **Eleanor Scott** (Highlands and Islands) speaks on health, rural development and marine issues.

Source: www.scottishgreens.org.uk

---

in the Scottish Parliament, Swinburne is also a member of the Finance Committee.

On policy matters, the SSCUP argues that senior citizens in Scotland should be entitled to a basic pension of £160 per week. This enhancement is vitally important to them as they claim that a third of Scotland's pensioners are living in poverty because the United Kingdom falls well behind the European average so far as state financial provision for pensioners. To try to redress the balance, the SSCUP campaigns against any form of '**means testing**' to establish entitlement. Allied to this campaign, the SSCUP has also put forward proposals for replacing the council tax with a local income tax that would be designed to be more favourable to those on lower incomes, include many pensioners. To benefit senior citizens further the SSCUP has advocated introducing schemes that will allow for a 50 per cent reduction in road tax and television licences for all pensioners.

The SSCUP also maintains that more residential and nursing homes need to be introduced, now and in the future, to cater for Scotland's ageing population. In the first instance, the party also contends that existing residential and nursing homes should be given substantially increased funding by the Scottish Executive. Another key demand from the SSCUP is the introduction of free national travel for all senior citizens. Some progress was made on this demand with the introduction, on 1 April 2006, of free bus and coach travel for senior citizens – defined as those people who are sixty and over – within Scotland. The bus scheme was expected to cost £159 million in 2006–7 rising to £163 million in 2007–8.

Citing the success of the Pensioners Party in Israel, who now hold the balance of power in the Israeli Knesset, the SSCUP seeks to attain the maximum number of votes and seats at the 2007 Scottish Parliamentary Election so that, as the party sees it, it can then compel the Scottish Executive to take more seriously the concerns of senior citizens.

Scottish political parties: the future

The first hurdle for every political party in Scotland to face up to is the 2007 Scottish Parliament Election. While the possibility of Scottish Labour and the Scottish Liberal Democrats continuing their coalition appears high, events outside Scotland could influence the Scottish electorate. For example, the decline in popularity that the Labour Party has endured at a UK level, with question marks hanging over the New Labour leadership and some of the party's policies, such as its strategy in Iraq, could sway some Scottish voters to seek alternatives.

Whichever party, or parties, benefit from a decline in Labour support depends upon the following factors:

- The ideological preference of the individual voter. For instance, people with socialist beliefs could drift to the Scottish Socialist Party while those with more nationalistic views may opt for the SNP.
- The manifestos of the political parties. Issues such as the National Health Service (NHS) are seen as being 'high priority' in people's eyes. The party with the most inventive, or most practical, solution to solving some of the problems of the NHS may see an increase in its support.

- The party leaders have to perform under the glare of the Scottish and world media. While the First Minister, Jack McConnell, has to deal with intense questioning on a daily basis, other party leaders do not routinely have to undergo such detailed scrutiny. If one of these other leaders can handle the pressure and impress the voters, then his or her party may gain significantly.

Whatever the outcome of the 2007 Scottish Parliament Election, and subsequent elections, devolution has helped to shape and transform Scottish politics, and Scottish political parties, for generations to come. Box 6.5 (below) gives some indications of the ways in which

---

Box 6.5 The Steel Commission and the future for Scottish devolution (March 2006)

- Devolution in Scotland has helped to create a framework for greater policy freedom and innovative ideas.
- There is evidence of public support for the devolution process and for additional powers to be granted to the Scottish Parliament.
- In international terms, Scotland compares favourably with the decentralised political systems operating in comparable countries. Nevertheless, Britain remains one of the most centralised fiscal states in the developed world.
- A new Constitutional Convention should be established to review the powers of the Scottish Parliament.
- The Scottish Parliament should have exclusive competence over issues such as transport powers, energy policy and the operation of the civil service.
- There should be a new written constitution for the United Kingdom which entrenches the rights of Scotland within a new constitutional framework.
- The term 'Scottish Executive' should be replaced by 'Scottish Government'.
- The Scotland Office should be abolished and replaced by a UK Department of the Nations and Regions.
- The Scottish Parliament should be given responsibility for all taxes except for those reserved to the United Kingdom. Hence moves towards 'fiscal federalism' should be considered.

Source: www.scotlibdems.org.uk

devolution may change in the years ahead if the 101-page report of the Steel Commission, chaired by former Presiding Officer, David Steel, is acted upon. As mentioned in the previous chapter, the Scottish political system, was already markedly different from that operating in other parts of Britain. As the United Kingdom becomes more decentralised, then this process of individual national identity and unique political arrangements will continue and expand. It is likely, given these circumstances, that in the years ahead the electorate may see the introduction of more political parties representing the left, right, and centre of Scottish political opinion.

....

✔ What you should have learnt from reading this chapter

- Scotland's political landscape differs from that of other parts of Britain.
- Since devolution, Scotland has moved from a four-party system of governance to a seven-party system.
- Devolution has forced parties, like Labour and the Conservatives, to become more Scottish in their thinking and in their public personas.
- Devolution has, arguably, given more voice to previously peripheral issues and peripheral political parties.
- There is still a debate about how far down the devolutionary road the Scottish people wish to go.

🔎 Glossary of key terms

Big bang The theory, supported by many fundamentalists within the SNP, that Scotland would achieve independence in a swift, almost revolutionary, manner following a huge pro-SNP vote in an election.

Centre ground The area on the political spectrum that is inhabited by people of a liberal or social-democratic persuasion. Sometimes referred to as 'the middle-of-the-road'.

Democratic socialism The ideological position of the Scottish Socialist Party. Democratic socialists want a socialist society to come about through democratic, parliamentary methods rather than through violent revolution.

Environmentalism The belief in preserving and enhancing the natural world. Although environmentalism is most commonly associated with the Scottish Green Party, other parties also like to present themselves as 'environmentally friendly'.

Four nations model The argument that any talk of the United Kingdom must take account of the four nations that comprise it. Therefore, there must be some acknowledgement that each has its own history and culture that distinguish it from being just 'British'.

Fundamentalist A faction within the Scottish National Party (SNP) that wants independence immediately after the SNP achieves electoral success in Scotland. Fundamentalists are generally suspicious about the efficacy of the devolution process.

Gradualist Gradualists within the SNP believe in an evolutionary road to self-government that passes through the devolutionary avenue. The gradualist vision has been the predominant view in the SNP in recent years.

Localist A belief that local, or community-based, political issues should be foremost on the agenda.

Means testing System of measurement, normally financial, that is used by officers of the state, such as civil servants, to determine whether or not somebody is entitled to a benefit.

New Labour The label associated with the Labour Party since its move to the right under Tony Blair. Many activists in Scottish Labour seek to distance themselves from the New Labour tag.

Political collectivism The idea that issues are best dealt with in a group rather than on an individual basis. The principle of the National Health Service (NHS) is a good example of this collectivist approach.

Pragmatic nationalists Label given to the Scottish Labour Party as it sought to show its commitment to Scotland while maintaining its British identity and its 'British' social-policy agenda.

? Likely examination questions

Discuss the ways in which the Scottish political scene is unique within the United Kingdom.

Is it fair to claim that, when it comes to the issue of devolution, most voters in Scotland would describe themselves as 'gradualist' rather than 'fundamentalist'?

Account for the rise of the Scottish Socialists since devolution.

Explain how the voting system used in elections for the Scottish Parliament has aided the political fortunes of the Greens in Scotland.

Examine the reasons behind the relative success of the Scottish Senior Citizens Unity Party.

🖥 Helpful websites

www.scottishlabour.org.uk The Scottish Labour Party.

www.scotlibdems.org.uk The Scottish Liberal Democrats.

www.snp.org The SNP (Scottish National Party).

www.scottishconservatives.com The Scottish Conservative Party.

www.scottishsocialistparty.org The Scottish Socialist Party.

www.scottishgreens.org.uk The Scottish Green Party.

www.sscup.org The Scottish Senior Citizens Unity Party.

📚 Suggestions for further reading

G. Hassan, *The Scottish Labour Party*, Edinburgh University Press, 2004.

P. Lynch, *Scottish Government and Politics: An Introduction*, Edinburgh University Press, 2001.

P. Lynch, *SNP: The History of the Scottish National Party*, Welsh Academic Press, 2002.

CHAPTER 7

The Government of Wales

Contents

Overview

Despite political devolution, most government services in Wales are still regulated directly from London (Westminster and Whitehall). All primary legislation originates in Westminster, and a large amount of government spending in Wales is determined centrally in Whitehall (pensions, social security and law and order). Devolution in the form of the National Assembly for Wales (Welsh Assembly) has, however, changed the way Wales is governed to a significant degree. The Welsh Assembly is referred to as an executive model of devolution; this is distinct from the administrative model used by the Welsh Office or the legislative/parliamentary model seen in the Scottish Parliament. It has brought an increased 'localism' in the way that politics is now undertaken in Wales. This chapter therefore examines the way in which Wales is governed centrally on an all-Wales level. It examines how devolution developed and the modern-day operation of the National Assembly for Wales (Welsh Assembly). The chapter also looks briefly at the interaction between Wales and the European Union.

Key issues to be covered in this chapter

- The origins of political and administrative devolution in Wales
- The problems with the former role of Westminster and Whitehall in the government of Wales prior to devolution
- How Westminster now relates to Wales in the post-devolution era
- The role of the First Minister and the Welsh cabinet
- How Wales relates to the European Union in the devolution era

The road to devolution in Wales

Wales was never really one unified nation in the form that we know today. Welsh princes, such as Llewellyn and Owain Glyn Dwr, succeeded in uniting some parts of Wales under one leadership but this never included the whole nation. It was Henry VIII, therefore, who united the public-administration systems of Wales and England under the Acts of Union (1536–42). From the mid-sixteenth century onwards, the administration of Wales was gradually integrated fully into that of England. It then evolved as an element of the English administrative system. In the centuries that followed, the links between England and Wales were strengthened by 'physical proximity, population movement and common legal and educational systems'. It was not until the last half of the nineteenth century that a Welsh national consciousness developed to such an extent, through the Welsh National Liberals and the *Cymru Fydd* (Young Wales) movement, that the status quo was challenged. The Liberal governments provided greater administrative devolution to Wales, such as the establishment of the Welsh Boards of Education and Health, but the more general desire for a Welsh parliament, as part of '**Home Rule all round**', and substantial administrative devolution did not occur.

Despite the numerous attempts to bring substantive administrative devolution to Wales, it took seventy-two years from the first attempt to create a Welsh Secretary in Parliament in 1892, until the Labour government eventually did so in 1964. The Conservative Party, and for many years the Labour Party, were always thoroughly opposed to the establishment of a Welsh Secretary or a Welsh Office. All attempts to establish them were rebuffed by the parties. The main obstacle in the decentralisation of administrative authority from London to Cardiff was that, unlike Ireland and Scotland, Wales lacked any widespread tradition of being treated as a separate administrative unit. The Conservatives, the Labour Party and the Home Civil Service (whose headquarters are based in Whitehall, London) resented a division of authority on an area or national basis, and always stressed the advantages of unified administrative control.

Eventually it was the Labour Party that was persuaded of the virtues of administrative devolution by those within their own

Welsh ranks. In 1964 Labour won the general election and a Welsh Office was established, with Welsh Labour elder statesman James Griffiths becoming the first Welsh Secretary in recognition of his continued pro-devolutionary campaigning. It had been a bitter battle within the Labour Party and was to foreshadow that which would occur later over political devolution in Wales. From now on, however, Wales would at least have its own secretary of state – who, in theory, would project the Welsh voice into the cabinet and government.

The development of the Welsh Office

Between its foundation in 1964 and its demise in 1999, the Welsh Office represented the most obvious example of the devolution of public administration to Wales. Over the thirty-five years of its existence, the Welsh Office grew from a territorial government ministry, with mainly executive oversight responsibilities (commenting on the work of the other government departments), to a department with its own functional remit. Over the course of its existence, the Welsh Office grew tenfold in the number of civil servants employed within it. The size of its budget and its powers also grew considerably. It always, however, remained weaker in terms of staffing, ministerial complement and range of functions compared with its sister departments in Northern Ireland and Scotland. In 1978, in response to the forthcoming devolution referendum, the funding of the Welsh Office was fixed. The Welsh Office was given a fixed sum each year, known as the Welsh Block. Any additional money to this was supplied under what became known as the Barnett Formula.

In its first twenty years, the Welsh Office was run by Welsh secretaries who had come from Wales and who tried to shape it to meet Welsh circumstances. In 1987, however, the Conservatives could no longer find any suitable MPs from Wales and, from then on, it was run by English MPs. This was just one of the problems with the operation of the Welsh Office (see Box 7.1).

The problems of the Welsh Office in turn led to greater demands for a Welsh assembly and to a series of events that led to its eventual establishment (see Box 7.2).

Box 7.1 What was wrong with the Welsh Office?

The problems with the role of Westminster and Whitehall in the government of Wales were:

1. The Welsh Office was Whitehall's smallest ministry and was therefore at the bottom of the ministerial pecking order. This meant that the Welsh Office was always the junior partner in ministerial negotiations.
2. The Welsh population constantly voted against a Conservative government yet, for most of the existence of the Welsh Office, it was a Conservative government that ran Wales and the Welsh Office.
3. Many of the Welsh Secretaries did not come from Wales. Only one of the six Conservative Welsh Secretaries held a seat in Wales. Conservative Welsh Secretaries tended to be there for a short time before trying their hand at moving their way up the ministerial/political ladder though their fortunes in doing so were mixed.
4. Wales under the Welsh Office was run by a vast bureaucracy in the shape of the Welsh quangos. These quangos became bigger than the democratically elected Welsh local authorities. They were responsible for the allocation of billions of pounds of government money yet remained responsible to only a few government ministers.
5. Whitehall and Westminster were heavily congested with government business which meant that they had little time to spend on necessary Welsh legislation and business.

Box 7.2 Important events on the road to a Welsh assembly

- From 1888 to 1979 numerous attempts to bring in a Welsh parliament failed. The 1979 St David's Day referendum for a Welsh assembly was defeated by five to one.
- The 1983 General Election manifestos of the Welsh Liberal/SDP and Plaid Cymru made it clear that both political parties still supported the idea of a Welsh parliament.
- From 1979 to 1987 Labour ignored the issue of political devolution for Wales. In 1987 they lost the general election, which caused them to re-examine the concept of a Welsh assembly.

- In May 1987 future prominent Labour figures Jon Owen Jones and Rhodri Morgan were elected as Labour MPs. Rhodri Morgan became a member and Jon Owen Jones the Chairman of the Campaign for a Welsh Assembly. Their drive pushed the issue of a Welsh assembly further up the Labour Party agenda.
- In October 1987 a working group was appointed by the Labour Party to look at the future of local government in Wales. When it reported back in 1989, it recommended the establishment of a Welsh assembly.
- In their 1992 General Election manifestos the Labour Party, Plaid Cymru and the Liberal Democrats all stated they would establish a Welsh assembly/parliament.
- In 1994 the Wales Labour Party established a Constitutional Policy Commission which produced a series of reports over the following years, endorsed by conference, which detailed how the Welsh assembly would be run.
- In 1996 Ron Davies, Shadow Welsh Secretary, announced the new assembly would be elected by a PR system, and would be introduced only after a referendum.
- In March 1997 Ron Davies, the Labour 'leader' in Wales, and Alex Carlile, the Welsh Liberal Democrat leader, signed a joint declaration committing both parties top campaign for a yes vote in any referendum.
- In May 1997 the Labour Party won the general election. In July they published a White Paper, *A Voice for Wales*, which detailed the nature of the new assembly.
- The Welsh assembly referendum was held on 18 September 1997. Half the Welsh counties voted no but the numerical superiority of the other eleven allowed a narrow majority for yes. The final vote was 50.3 per cent yes and 49.7 per cent no, with just over half of the Welsh electorate voting.
- In July 1998 the Government of Wales Act gained Royal Assent. The only major difference between the Act and the White Paper, *A Voice for Wales*, is that the assembly would now be run on a cabinet system instead of the previous model designed on local government committees.
- In May 1999 the first elections to the assembly were held. Labour gained twenty-eight seats, Plaid Cymru seventeen, Conservatives nine and Liberal Democrats six. Alun Michael became the First Minister and Lord Dyfydd Elis Thomas its Presiding Officer.

Wales at Westminster

As the assembly does not currently have its own primary law-making powers, the parliament at Westminster remains very important in the political life of Wales. There have been very few purely Welsh acts made within parliament. Wales does not have a separate legal system from England. Therefore, the main Welsh role of Welsh MPs in Westminster concerns the process of the keeping the executive (government) in check. All of the main political parties in Britain are represented in Wales (see Box 7.3). The most regular opportunity for Welsh involvement is at the parliamentary question times attended by the Welsh Secretary and his/her junior minister. Held every three to four weeks, this method became more limited after devolution by concerning only non-devolved assembly issues.

Westminster politics in Wales is quite different from that concerning the Welsh Assembly. Traditionally, it has suffered from two democratic flaws.

The first concerns the lack of female MPs, until 1997 there had only ever been four female Welsh MPs. Since then, however, the Labour Party's use of **all-women short-lists**, and the success of the Welsh Liberal Democrats in gaining a female member for Cardiff Central (Jenny Willott), have reduced this severe gender imbalance. After the 2005 General Election, however, only 20 per cent of the seats in Wales were held by women.

The second flaw concerns the over-representation of the Labour Party compared with its share of the votes. Under the first-past-the-post electoral system, Wales has one of the most imbalanced electoral systems in the Western world. Between 1970 and 2001 Labour gained between 35 and 55 per cent of the vote but never less than 63 per cent, and as much as 85 per cent, of the total Westminster seats. This disadvantages the other political parties in Wales at election time.

In contrast to Westminster, the Welsh Assembly is an evenly balanced legislature in terms of its gender balance, and the proportionality of its votes gained per party to seats won is also much more balanced than those at Westminster elections.

Over the last fifty years, Westminster has evolved to allow a broader input from Welsh MPs on purely Welsh matters. The first

Box 7.3 The Welsh political parties at Westminster

Just like MPs in the rest of the United Kingdom, those in Wales play numerous roles at Westminster. All the political parties, with the exception of the Conservatives, operate Welsh parliamentary groups. The Wales Labour Party is the main political group of MPs in Wales, and a number of these MPs serve in the government. The most prominent of these members in Labour's first three governments, formed after 1997, have been Peter Hain whose posts have included, Secretary of State for Wales and Leader of the House of Commons. Then he became Northern Ireland Secretary and Secretary of State for Wales. Also, Paul Murphy was Leader of the House of Commons, Secretary of State for Northern Ireland, and Secretary of State for Wales. Under the Labour governments between 1997 and 2005, a Welsh presence was re-established in the cabinet after a ten-year absence under the Conservatives. Welsh-born politicians who also held a seat in Wales, however, remained a rarity in Tony Blair's government.

The Conservatives, with no MPs in Wales between 1997 and 2005, have had no prominent Welsh MPs in the post-devolution era. Their shadow Welsh secretaries have all represented English seats and, until 2005, were not in the shadow cabinet. In December 2005, they appointed their first female Shadow Welsh Secretary, Cheryl Gillan, the MP for Chesham and Amersham since April 1992. Like most of their former Welsh secretaries, she had little connection with Wales. Although she had been born in Cardiff, her education and subsequent career took place in England.

After May 2005, the Welsh Liberal Democrats, with four MPs in Wales, became the official opposition in Wales. Lembit Opik (their longest-serving Welsh MP whose name is of Estonian origin) became the Shadow Welsh and the Shadow Northern Ireland Secretary in a mirror to cabinet in London. The Welsh Liberal Democrat MPs link up with their parliamentary colleagues from Scotland and England for all non-devolved issues.

Plaid Cymru has just three MPs, all in Wales. Each of its MPs was Welsh born and, like the Conservatives, the party has never had a female MP in Wales. Elfyn Llwyd is the party's leader in the House of Commons. The Plaid Cymru MPs form a single parliamentary grouping together with their Scottish National Party colleagues at Westminster, following a formal pact signed in 1986. This enables Plaid Cymru to 'punch above its weight' at Westminster (see Box 7.6).

modern step into accepting that Wales was a political entity in its own right occurred in 1946 when the Leader of the House, Herbert Morrison, introduced an annual Welsh Day debate. This still occurs on around St David's Day (1 March) each year. In 1960 a Welsh Grand Committee was established; it incorporated all the Welsh MPs supplemented by others. Today, it meets to discuss, among other things, Welsh legislation.

The most important committee in Westminster concerned with Wales is the Select Committee on Welsh Affairs, established in 1979. Following the arrival of the Welsh Assembly, the committee was given a wider remit covering any government policy in Wales not being undertaken by the assembly. When it deals with issues related to the assembly, the committee liaises closely with it. It has established a way of working through consultation, visits and appearing before assembly committees.

Westminster and the Welsh Assembly

When the assembly was established, seven Welsh MPs and one Welsh Lord also became members of the Welsh Assembly. By the time of the second term of the Welsh Assembly, only two assembly members had been MPs, and one Lord (Dafydd Elis Thomas) remained. In the General Election of May 2005, two assembly members were elected to Westminster, thus reversing the process started by Westminster MPs in going to Cardiff in 1999.

Because the Welsh Assembly had no primary legislative power, the government made it clear that it would not reduce the number of Welsh MPs. Welsh MPs were still needed to take part in primary law-making for issues affecting the Welsh Assembly. This is also in part because the Labour government is aware that it needs to retain its traditional South Wales Labour constituencies if it is to continue to form governments at Westminster.

Westminster currently comes into contact with the assembly in the following ways:

1. The *dual mandate*. A number of Welsh **AM**s have been or are MPs or Lords at the same time. This gives them contact with both bodies.

2. The *Liaison Committee of the House of Commons*. This is a committee of MPs which meets regularly with members of the assembly to discuss issues of common interest.

3. The Welsh Assembly has a *Legislation Committee* which partially deals with forthcoming primary legislation at Westminster. To a limited degree this shadows bills at Westminster.

4. The *British-Irish Council (Council of the Isles)*. Here the Wales assembly government mixes with members of the governments of the Scottish and Irish parliaments, Northern Ireland Assembly (when it sits) and the Westminster government.

5. The *liaison between the Welsh Secretary and the Welsh Assembly*. Although the Welsh Secretary's main powers,(see Box 7.4) and duties have been passed on to the assembly, the post remains, albeit combined with that of Leader of the House. It is the Welsh Secretary who consults the assembly on the Westminster government's legislative programme.

The National Assembly for Wales – Cynulliad Cenedlaethol Cymru

The Welsh Assembly is a single-chamber body, quasi-**unicameral**, as opposed to the Westminster parliament which has two tiers, the House of Commons and the House of Lords (**bicameral**). The Welsh Assembly took over the majority of the rights, powers and duties of the Welsh Secretary. It has wide-ranging powers. The former Welsh Office defined the main powers of the assembly in 1998.

• To make rules and regulations (subordinate legislation) which expand on Acts of Parliament (primary legislation) and gives more detail. There are more than 300 Acts of Parliament under which the Welsh Assembly has the power to make rules and regulations. Around 400 new Statutory Instruments are issued by the assembly each year. Under this delegated legislation, the assembly, for example, can define the content of the National Curriculum in Wales.

• To make appointments to the Welsh quangos. The chairs and boards of public bodies, such as the NHS Health Trusts, are now appointed by the Welsh Assembly.

Box 7.4 The role of the Welsh Secretary

In June 2003 the cabinet post of Welsh Secretary was combined with that of Leader of the House (the government's parliamentary business manager). At the same time, the civil servants in the Wales Office were placed under the administrative and financial responsibility of the newly established Department for Constitutional Affairs (DCA). Although this means that the Wales Office (successor to the Welsh Office) is now technically under the control of the DCA, it is the Welsh Secretary and his or her junior minister who control the day-to-day running of the office.

The change was seen by some as a recognition that the centre of political power in respect of a number of important Welsh issues had now shifted from London to Cardiff. Others, however, felt that, without the necessary transfer of primary law-making power to Cardiff, Wales's voice in the cabinet was being weakened.

Under the new government arrangements two government ministers remain responsible for Wales. The Welsh Secretary and a junior minister. The first of the part-time Welsh secretaries was Peter Hain. Because the Welsh Assembly is not as powerful as the Scottish Parliament, his role remains important to the development of the new assembly. His duties are defined in part under the Government of Wales Act 1998. The main ones are as follows:

1. attends and speaks at sessions of the National Assembly;
2. ensures that the interests of Wales are fully considered in the workings of the British government;
3. steers Welsh primary legislation through parliament;
4. has functions relating to the fact that the House of Commons votes the Welsh Assembly's money to the Welsh Secretary who then makes a grant to the assembly after deciding the cost of running the Wales Office;
5. responsibility to consult the assembly on the government's legislative programmes;
6. responsibility to ensure that the arrangements for co-operation with the British government are working effectively.

- To spend the Welsh block. The assembly will have discretion to allocate its budget between its responsibilities. This is currently worth some £14 billion per year (2006).

- To acquire land and property, and to undertake works, such as the building of new roads.
- To decide upon disputes and appeals, such as those relating to planning inspections.

Before May 2007 the Welsh Assembly did not have a defined mechanism for have primary law-making powers (it could not create its own acts). It still has no tax-raising powers. This meant that the assembly had to govern by using what is called secondary legislation. This secondary legalisation comes from original (primary) Acts of the Westminster Parliament. It is through secondary legislation (Statutory Instruments) that an Act is enacted, developed or applied to particular Welsh circumstances. For Wales, the legislation often allows a lot of freedom for the Welsh Assembly government in its implementation. Often, an Act will leave it up to the Welsh Assembly as to whether or not the legislation is implemented at all.

The Welsh general election

The Government of Wales Act 1998 states clearly that the Welsh General Election (assembly election) must be held on the first Thursday in May every four years (it can be delayed, however, in the event of a royal death, until after the funeral). There are sixty AMs in the Welsh Assembly. Forty of these AMs are elected in the Welsh Westminster constituencies in the same way that the Westminster MPs are elected. This method of electoral selection is called '**first past the post**'. To ensure that the percentage of seats won in the assembly are closer to the actual percentage of votes cast for each party, a method of proportional representation, known as the additional member system (AMS), has been introduced. For this purpose, Wales is divided into five regions. In each of these regions there are four regional AMs from the regional lists. The parties can put up to twelve members on the lists. The way they choose their list members varies from party to party but it is normally through a ballot of the parties' Welsh members in the region concerned. The Government of Wales Act 2006 forbids candidates from standing in both a constituency and on the regional list. This makes the Welsh AMS system different from that anywhere else in the world. In the 1999 assembly elections, the non-Labour political parties won nineteen of the twenty Assembly Members' seats. First Minister, Alun Michael, was the only Labour Party member to win a list seat. The AMS system is not as proportional as it is in Scotland. It did not allow any political party, other than the main four, to win a seat. It was, however, far more proportional than any other electoral method used in Wales.

The First Minister

The assembly is led by a first minister (originally called the first secretary) who is also the leader of the majority party in the assembly. The leader is the most powerful of all of the assembly members. At Welsh Assembly's commencement, the First Minister and the Welsh Secretary were the same man, Alun Michael. This was undertaken in order to maintain continuity in the government's running of Wales in its initial stages. It is the first minister who is the public face of the Welsh Assembly and the dynamo which keeps the assembly running. It is a vital role (see Box 7.5).

Box 7.5 The role of the First Minister

The role of the First Minister is:

- To lead the Assembly.
- To be the head of the Welsh Assembly Government.
- To liaise with the Welsh Secretary and Prime Minister over issues of governance.
- To lead and select the Assembly cabinet (executive committee).
- To liaise with the Secretary of State for Wales (and other Whitehall ministers as necessary) on policy and draft legislation relevant to assembly functions or to Wales more generally.
- To act as leader of the party in the assembly in wales.
- To ensure that the party's assembly manifesto is implemented.
- To take a lead in promoting AMs and selecting the members of the cabinet.
- To represent the assembly in European institutions and overseas.
- To hold regular question times within the assembly for Assembly Members.

The cabinet of the Welsh Assembly government (Welsh Executive)

The Welsh Executive's cabinet is the main decision-maker in the assembly's policy direction. It is also the main determinator of how government in Wales is run on a day-to-day basis. The cabinet can meet in private or public, as it wishes, but normally meets in private. The standing orders (rules) for the Welsh Assembly state that the Welsh cabinet can not have more than nine members including the First Minister. There are also four deputy ministers who do not sit in the cabinet. The First Minister selects the cabinet shortly after the own appointment of the deputy ministers following the Welsh general election. If the government is a coalition, as occurred between 2000 and 2003, then the other political party or parties nominate their own ministers whose portfolios are negotiated with the First Minister. Cabinet members are chosen on the basis of:

1. their interest in doing the jobs;
2. tenure and experience as an Assembly Member;
3. a balance between male and female;
4. their geographical location (which area of Wales they represent).

Ministers have not always been appointed with due consideration for the posts concerned. There was considerable upset in the farming community when Alun Michael appointed Christine Gwyther as Agriculture Minister. Welsh farming is concerned mainly with livestock (meat) production yet Gwyther was a vegetarian. In 1999, Tom Middlehurst, who was appointed to be the minister in charge of the Welsh language, was unable to speak or read Welsh, nor was his successor Jenny Randerson.

Of the cabinet secretaries, that of the Economic Development Minister, responsible for employment and business-promotion issues in Wales, is the most important ministerial post. The first holder of this post was Rhodri Morgan MP, the twice-failed Wales Labour leadership contender. His appointment was seen as a consolation prize for his failed leadership bids. The Business Minister is the second most important post, holding the same status as the Leader of House of Commons combined with that of Chief Whip. The

Business Minister has to ensure that the government's business agenda goes through smoothly and on time. The assembly ministers hold regular question times within the assembly, just as in Westminster, where Assembly Members can ask them oral or written questions. With the exception of the Business Minister and First Minister, each cabinet minister is also a member of the assembly committee appropriate to his/her remit. Thus, the Environment Minister sits on the Environment Committee and this is repeated for the other respective ministers.

The committees

The assembly cabinet does not enjoy total freedom of action. The full assembly's approval, for instance, is required for the cabinet's recommendations on the budget allocation between programmes. From May 2007 the assembly was able to 'vote' for the assembly budget to be 'drawn down' from Westminster. If it fails to do so then the Welsh Assembly government cannot continue to operate. The assembly committees also play important roles, as they comprise the mechanism by which ordinary Assembly Members can play a regular part in the scrutiny and development of policy in the assembly.

The committee chairs and members for the non-regional committees are appointed in proportion to the parties' political strengths within the assembly. The four regional committees, based on four economic areas, contain all of the Assembly Members representing that region. This means, therefore, that it is unlikely that they are proportional to the balance of the political parties in the assembly. Until 2007 committee chairs set the committees' agendas in consultation with the relevant cabinet member. After this date, however, ministers were no longer part of these committees. The committees have five main purposes:

1. reviewing the effectiveness of policies and helping develop new policies;
2. scrutinising and reviewing the work of bodies funded by the assembly;
3. scrutinising, debating and amending secondary legislation;

4. discussing Westminster and European legislation which affects their particular committee;
5. passing their views on to the cabinet.

The similarities between Westminster and the Welsh Assembly

The rationale behind the assembly was in part that it was meant to be a modern democratic body which did not have any of the drawbacks of Westminster. The assembly therefore lacks the pomp and circumstance of Westminster. For example, members are not referred to as 'The Honourable' or 'Right Honourable Member for Cardiff North', but instead are referred to simply by their first names or surnames. The assembly chamber is set in a 'horseshoe' shape and each Assembly Member has his/her own desk with a computer terminal on it. The parties therefore sit facing the Presiding Officer and not one another as they do at Westminster.

Unlike at Westminster, the Assembly Members vote by computer voting but, as at Westminster, their votes can be recorded only if they are actually in the chamber. There is also a verbatim record, called *The Record*, of the assembly and its committees. The Assembly is also fully bilingual as speeches can be made in English or Welsh (full simultaneous translation facilities exist for this purpose). Other similarities to Westminster include the committee system and the cabinet ministers' question times with their written and oral questions. The list of similarities is shown in Table 7.1.

Not everything in the assembly has proved to be better or more popular than Westminster is. In the debates in the assembly, for instance, members do not have to 'give way' to other members when making a speech. This practice is prevalent in the House of Commons where MPs are obliged to let other MPs comment on their speech at anytime during its course. In the assembly, members can talk uninterrupted but it also means that there can be no room for the opposition to have its say. From 1999 onwards, Plaid Cymru has been the second largest political party in the Welsh Assembly. Just as the Welsh Assembly has, Plaid Cymru has also been evolving since 1999 (see Box 7.6).

Table 7.1 Common terms: how the Welsh Assembly translates to Westminster

Westminster	Welsh Assembly
Prime Minister	First Minister
Speaker	Presiding Officer
Chancellor	Finance Minister
Leader of the House, Chief Whip	Business Minister
Erskin May	Standing Orders
Hansard	The Record
Leader of the Opposition	Post or position does not officially exist but, since 1999, it has been regarded as the assembly government's opposition
Official Opposition	Technically all opposition are treated equally but Labour and Plaid Cymru have established a government–opposition system

Wales and the European Union

Wales's position in the European Union is vital for its economic future. Wales benefits considerably from European funding. Over the last two decades, the Welsh economy has declined in comparison with other European Union regions, as it shifted from its traditional reliance on coal and steel to more modern industries. In 1999 a large part of Wales was declared **Objective 1** by the European Union. This brought in over a billion pounds, worth of European aid but did not produce the European-inspired economic regeneration that had rebuilt the Irish economy. Much of Wales is also connected closely to the rural economy. Wales is, therefore, influenced by what occurs within the Common Agricultural Policy (CAP).

Box 7.6 Plaid Cymru loses the 'Cymru'

At its spring conference in 2006 Plaid Cymru undertook a series of radical changes to its image. The leadership, which had been split between two people, now reverted back to one, the party's assembly leader, Ieuan Wyn Jones. The party dropped its traditional triban logo which it had used since 1933. It consisted of three peaks representing what Plaid Cymru called its key values: self-government, cultural prosperity and economic prosperity. The triban emblem was replaced by a yellow Welsh poppy (*Meconopsis cambrica*), and the logo's green colour was changed to yellow. At the same time, Plaid Cymru dropped the word 'Cymru' from its branding but did retain its official name as 'Plaid Cymru – the Party of Wales'. Despite the change in name, Plaid has continued to be referred to as Plaid Cymru by the media and by many members of the party itself, so that is the name we have used in this book.

Plaid Cymru had been in political decline since 1999, losing control of councils, MPs and AMs. The change of branding was designed to try to modernise the party's image with the voters and to try to reverse its decline.

As well as its four members of the European Parliament (MEPs) Wales has a number of direct and indirect links with the European Union. In the context of the Welsh Assembly the foremost of these links are:

- The Welsh Secretary and First Minister, with the agreement of the leading British minister, can form part of the British delegation at the Council of Ministers. There they can ensure that the views of Wales are expressed in any meetings.
- The Welsh Assembly has an input to draft European legislation. This has developed since a member of the assembly's research service was based in Brussels and identifies forthcoming European legislation that could be of interest to the assembly and then notifies the relevant assembly committees which they then consider. The Legislation Committee, however, becomes involved with European legislation only once it has been made. The committee scrutinises statutory instruments made by the Welsh Assembly government which purport to be implementing

EC legislation to check that all the cross-references are correct, and that they do, indeed, implement EC obligations within the assembly's powers.

- The Welsh Assembly has a Committee on European and External Affairs which meets nine times year to discuss issues relating to Europe and to the wider world. This committee takes an overview of what is coming up in Brussels and looks in particular at issues that do not fall neatly within the responsibility of individual subject committees. This, together with the Welsh Assembly government's European and External Affairs' Division, are responsible for overseeing the administration of structural funds, co-ordinating European issues as they affect the assembly, and maintaining the assembly's office in Brussels.

- The assembly has at least one annual plenary debate on Wales in Europe. This allows the Assembly Members to debate the Welsh cabinet's handling of matters relating to the European Union.

- The European Commission Office and its representatives in Cardiff feed information and consultation directly to the Welsh Assembly and Wales.

- Welsh representation on the Committee of the Regions. Wales has two representatives from local government and the assembly on this European body for providing the European institutions with a local and regional point of view.

Conclusion

The road to devolution in Wales has been lengthy and far bumpier than that in Scotland. Administrative and political devolution has come only after years of hard campaigning within the Labour Party. The Welsh referendums on devolution in 1979 and 1997 combined multi-party support in favour of devolution for the first time in Wales. At the same time Wales's Westminster MPs have had to adjust to working in a post-devolution era.

✔ **What you should have learnt from reading this chapter**

- The fierce opposition to devolution in Wales took over a century to overcome. Initially this was led by the Conservative Party but later on the Labour Party followed suit.

- Despite being hostile to political devolution, the Conservatives and the Labour Party ensured that devolution developed in Wales. Both parties were instrumental in advancing administrative devolution through the Welsh Office, and the Labour Party was the key player in bringing forward political devolution to Wales in the form of the Welsh Assembly.

- In the twentieth century, Westminster politics in Wales suffered from a number of flaws including over-representation of the majority political parties and men, the undemocratic nature of the Welsh Office and the appointment of the Welsh secretaries. These have been only partially redressed by the establishment of the Welsh Assembly.

- The establishment of the Welsh Assembly was the result of a long process of campaigning and development within Wales, mainly within the Labour Party.

- Westminster has developed mechanisms to scrutinise and to develop legislation and policies specifically for Wales. Whitehall has also adapted to the arrival of the Welsh Assembly, and the post of Secretary of State for Wales has been reshaped accordingly.

- The National Assembly for Wales (Welsh Assembly) was established under a committee system based in part on a local-government model. Since 1999, however, it has been striving to become more like a parliament.

- The First Minister is the dominant political figure, not only in the Welsh Assembly but also in Welsh politics. He or she is the leader of the Welsh Assembly government and of the largest political party in Wales.

- Wales is not only connected with politics at Westminster, it is also closely linked with events taking place at the European Parliament and Commission.

🔎 **Glossary of key terms**

All-women shortlist policy The course of action undertaken by the Wales Labour Party where by seats in which the party has a successful track record in winning have their Labour Party candidate selection limited to female-only lists. It is designed to increase the number of female Labour MPs in Wales.

AM Assembly Member.

Bicameral A legislature with two chambers.

First past the post electoral system A system in which Wales is divided into geographical constituencies (council wards). The winner in each seat is the candidate who gains a simple majority on one or more votes.

Home Rule all round The name given in the early twentieth century to the Liberal government's policy of providing political devolution to all the nations in the British Isles to try to solve the problems of Ireland.

Objective 1 The European Union's description of an economic area where development is lagging behind. It allows for the highest level of funding to be given.

Official Opposition The name given to the largest elected opposition party.

Statutory Instrument The name given to the publication of delegated (secondary) legislation.

Unicameral A legislature (law-making body) with one chamber (group of elected members).

Likely examination questions

'The new devolved governments in Scotland and Wales are no more accountable than the former Scottish and Welsh Offices.' Critically examine this view of devolved government.

To what extent do Westminster and Whitehall still dominate political life in Wales?

Trace the key events that led to the establishment of the Welsh Assembly and indicate the extent to which its arrival was either a process of evolution or revolution?

Helpful websites

http://www.llgc.org.uk/ymgyrchu/map-e.htm The National Library of Wales has a substantial website on Welsh political history.

http://www.bbc.co.uk/wales/history/ BBC Wales history site – the web pages have a good coverage of Welsh history.

There is also a host of websites linked to academic institutions and political parties in Wales:

http://www.aber.ac.uk/interpol/IWP/ Institute of Welsh Politics.

http://www.iwa.org.uk/ Institute for Welsh Affairs (Welsh think tank).

www.wales.gov.uk National Assembly for Wales.

http://www.plaidcymru.org/ Plaid Cymru, The Party of Wales.

www.walesoffice.gov.uk Wales Office.

www.welshlabour.org.uk Wales Labour Party.

http://www.conservatives.com Welsh Conservatives.

http://www.welshlibdems.org.uk/home_e.asp Welsh Liberal Democrats.

Suggestions for further reading

J. Davies, *A History of Wales*, Penguin, 1994.

R. Deacon, *The Governance of Wales: The Welsh Office and the Policy Process 1964–99*, Welsh Academic Press, 2002.

P. Madgwick and D. Woodhouse, *The Law and Politics of the Constitution*, Harvester Wheatsheaf, 1995.

K. O. Morgan, *Wales in British Politics 1868–1922*, University of Wales Press, 1980.

National Assembly Advisory Group (1998) Recommendations, Welsh Office, August 1998.

CHAPTER 8

The Continuing Evolution of Welsh Devolution

Contents

Overview

The National Assembly for Wales was quick in finding its feet. Before long, the legislature had become commonly known as the Welsh Assembly, and the Executive had become the Welsh Assembly government. From now on both would help to shape policy and service delivery over areas ranging from agriculture and education to Welsh culture and language, and economic development. This chapter explores the development of the Welsh Assembly over its first two terms. The problems and successes of the Welsh Assembly, its leadership, the minority and coalition governments, and issues, such as the controversy surrounding the new assembly building, are examined. The assembly is an evolving institution, so those events that have been important in its evolution, such as Lord Richard's Commission into the future development of the Welsh Assembly and the subsequent Government of Wales Act 2006, are outlined. Two other important aspects of Wales, the Welsh language and issues surrounding Welsh culture, are also examined.

Key issues to be covered in this chapter

- The main developments at a Welsh government level occurring in the first two terms of the Welsh Assembly
- The fall of First Secretary Alun Michael and the rise of First Minister Rhodri Morgan
- The problems within the Wales Labour Party that led to its becoming a minority government
- The attempt to end the role of many Welsh quangos
- Moulding the assembly's future through the Richard Commission and the Government of Wales Act (2006)
- The Welsh language and threats to Welsh cultural identity

Consensus politics: the early years

When the Welsh Assembly was elected for the first time in 1999, no one party achieved an overall majority. The Wales Labour Party became the largest party with twenty-eight seats but that was three short of a majority. When the same situation occurred in Scotland, Labour and the Liberal Democrats formed a pact and governed together, but this did not occur in Wales. Instead, the Labour Party determined that it would rule alone, in what is called a 'minority government' (no one political party has a majority of the seats). It determined that it would govern Wales in future by trying to achieve a broad consensus with the other political parties over certain issues. The other political parties were not in a position to achieve government by themselves, and so a short period of consensus politics began in Wales as the political parties sought to adjust to the post-devolution political situation in Cardiff.

The Assembly Members met initially in a converted office block (Crickhowell House). It was thought at the time that this would be a temporary measure but it was to be another seven years before they moved into their new purpose-built chamber (see Box 8.1).

The consensus politics did not last long. On 20 October 1999 the assembly censured Agriculture Secretary, Christine Gwyther over her failure to secure a £750,000 aid package for Welsh dairy farmers. First Secretary, Alun Michael, refused to sack her and she refused to resign. This resulted in the Conservatives, under Nick Bourne, bringing a vote of no confidence against Alun Michael on 2 November 1999. The motion failed. Although Alun Michael had survived a no-confidence vote, the opposition now made it clear that they would unite over one issue concerning Europe. This concerned European Objective 1 funding to Wales and the need for the Treasury to supply 'matched funding' for Wales. The main issue was that the opposition wanted the Treasury to supply the money and not take it out of the assembly's existing grants. Pleas by Alun Michael to trust the Chancellor to deliver fell on stony ground, as did attempts by Michael to form a pact with the Welsh Liberal Democrats. When Plaid Cymru called a motion of no confidence in Alun Michael on the European issue again on 9 February 2000, Michael resigned and the motion was passed.

The resignation of Alun Michael was seen as the end of No. 10 Downing Street's attempts to micro-manage Welsh devolution as it

Box 8.1 Problems in building an assembly chamber

When it was decided that the new Welsh Assembly was to be based in Cardiff Bay, an architectural competition was held. Chaired by former Labour premier Lord Callaghan, it selected the design by the Richard Rogers Partnership (RRP), run by Lord Rogers. Originally, the costs for the project were set £12 million but, by November 2000, they had risen to £26.7 million. Later, the costs escalated from £37 million to £47 million. The eventual cost was around £67 million.

In July 2001, the RRP was dismissed from the project in a row over thesrising costs. After legal action, the partnership was later reinstated but the date for the new building was postponed until after the May 2003 assembly elections. The building had originally been due to be completed in April 2001, then it was to be January 2003, then September 2005, but it was not officially opened by the Queen until 1 March, St David's Day, 2006. The Welsh Assembly building opened five years late and cost more than five times the original estimate.

The new assembly building is referred to as the 'Senedd' building (Welsh for parliament), rather than 'Cynulliad' (Welsh for assembly). The name 'Senedd' caused some controversy and was opposed by those in the assembly who do wish to see it as a parliament.

resulted in Michael being replaced immediately by the very man Tony Blair least wanted to run Wales, Rhodri Morgan. Tony Blair had previously refused to transfer Morgan from his Shadow Welsh Office post into the Welsh Office itself, stating he was 'too old' for government. He had then campaigned against him when he had stood for the Welsh leadership. Now Rhodri Morgan was acting First Secretary. Within a week, he had been voted in as First Minister by the assembly, and was selected unopposed by the Labour Party as its Welsh Leader. Within a year Alun Michael would return to a junior ministerial post at Westminster and the assembly would remain under Rhodri Morgan's control.

Coalition had not come during Alun Michael's short tenure but, with Rhodri Morgan's arrival, talks between Labour and the Welsh Liberal Democrats began almost immediately. The partnership document, *Putting Wales First: A Partnership for the People of Wales,* was duly signed by both parties. The Welsh Liberal Democrats secured two cabinet posts. Michael German became Deputy First Minister and took over the Economic Development Secretary post. Welsh Liberal Democrat AM, Jenny Randerson, became Minister for Culture and Sports. At the same time, Randerson became the first ever female Liberal politician to hold office in a government anywhere in the United Kingdom. Some Labour members also lost their posts, and this would fuel future resentment within Labour ranks (see Box. 8.1). Tom Middlehurst resigned as Assembly Secretary for Post-16 Education and Training, technically because of his reservations about coalition, but he was also well aware that he was likely to be sacked to make way for the two new Liberal Democrat members. While these changes were going on, Rhodri Morgan also altered the name of First Secretary to First Minister, following the Scottish parliamentary model. At the same time, the cabinet secretaries also changed their titles to ministers.

Box 8.2 Welsh pressure groups and lobbyists

As much greater political power has been given to Cardiff, so the number of lobbyists and pressure groups has greatly increased. Under the old Welsh Office, a group of professional associations, mainly representing trade unions and local government, had concentrated around the Welsh Office's headquarters in Cathays Park. This became known as the 'Cathays Park Village'. When the Welsh Assembly arrived, the number of pressure groups and lobbyists grew substantially. They now centred around Cardiff Bay, where the assembly is located, forming a new 'Cardiff Bay Village'.

Most UK-wide charities have 'parliamentary officers' at the Welsh Assembly, as do trade unions, business organisations and professional lobbyists. Each of these groups has varying degrees of influence with the local government organisations, the Welsh Local Government Association perhaps exerting the most.

Wales has one main 'think tank' – the Institute for Welsh Affairs (IWA). The IWA produces a wealth of material and reports on the Welsh Assembly, and actively seeks to influence the policy agendas of all of the political parties, something which is not always welcomed by the ruling Welsh Government Executive.

The Labour-Liberal Democrat cabinet worked quite effectively together. The main problem for the coalition concerned the Welsh Liberal Democrat leader, Michael German. He had been forced to step down as Deputy Minister in July 2001 until police investigations into aspects of his previous role as an employee of the Welsh Joint Education committee (WJEC), particularly regarding various expenses claims, had been completed. Following the completion of those investigations, the Crown Prosecution Service issued a statement on 13 June 2002 stating that there was insufficient evidence to justify any criminal charges, and Mike German returned to the cabinet as both Deputy First Minister and Minister of Rural Development and Wales Abroad. It had, however, cast a shadow over the first year of the coalition government.

There was a general feeling among Welsh political observers that, in many areas, the Welsh Assembly had been very successful in shaping a distinctive Welsh policy agenda. The main dispute between the coalition partners in the first Welsh government was over who was responsible for the more popular policies. Just before the First Minister's second Annual Report in October 2002, Mike German, much to Labour's annoyance, claimed that six of the eight leading achievements of the assembly government that year had come directly from the Liberal Democrat manifesto. This did nothing to help ease Labour AMs' fears about entering into another coalition if they did not gain a majority in the 2003 assembly elections. When the elections did come, the Labour Party won exactly half the seats. This time, despite what had occurred with the minority government between 1999 and 2000, the bulk of the party again preferred to form a minority government which would be able to carry forward fully its own policy agenda until the May 2005 General Election. At this election a Labour AM, Peter Law, who had failed to be selected for the Westminster seat in Blaenau Gwent when the Labour Party imposed an all-women shortlist for the seat, stood as an Independent and won. Law was expelled from the party with some vitriol which meant that he now voted with the assembly opposition. The opposition's first major defeat of the Labour Welsh Assembly government occurred in a debate on university tuition fees on 24 May 2005. Assembly Members voted by thirty to twenty-nine in favour of a Welsh Conservative motion not to introduce top-up fees in Wales. After this defeat, the opposition knew that, if it was united, it could defeat the Welsh Assembly government on any issue at any time. From now on the opposition would defeat that assembly government whenever it felt strongly enough on an issue (see Box 8.3). In order to stay in power the Welsh Assembly government had now to gain agreement with the opposition over policy implementation. Once more, a period of 'forced' consensus government had come to the assembly. In simple terms, if the Welsh Assembly government could not achieve some form of consensus on its policy agenda, then it would fail.

Box 8.3 Welsh quangos go on the bonfire

While in opposition, the Wales Labour Party, Plaid Cymru and the Welsh Liberal Democrats complained bitterly about the rise in public life of the Welsh quangos or, as they were known in Wales, assembly-sponsored public bodies (**ASPB**s). The Wales Labour Party promised that, when it came to power, there would be a 'bonfire of the quangos'. When Labour gained power in 1997, it merged a few quangos into the Welsh Office but the vast majority remained untouched until after the 2003 assembly elections. In 2004, however, the Welsh Assembly government changed its policy on ASPBs. In July 2004, Rhodri Morgan announced that three of the largest quangos, the Welsh Development Agency, Wales Tourist Board and Education and Learning Wales (ELWa), would cease to exist by 2006. It later announced that it would take over many of the duties of a number of Wales's culture, sport and countryside ASPBs. In future funding would come directly from the assembly, rather than at 'arms length' from the ASPBs. In the assembly, the opposition, which had often noted the Welsh Assembly Government's failure to bring the ASPBs under more direct control, was taken aback by the speed of this proposed integration. They were also concerned about the loss of their own scrutiny powers over these bodies, and the fact that the assembly government would now have too much direct control over funding.

Although the political opposition didn't stop some of the larger ASPBs from being scrapped, they did force the Welsh Assembly Government to postpone the scrapping of the Welsh Language Board in October 2005. In addition, when it came to the issue of ending the role of the Arts Council for Wales in funding, opposition parties now claimed that this would breach the principle of 'arms-length' funding of the arts and blocked this move as well.

Creating the Welsh Assembly's future: the Richard Commission

We have seen how the assembly is in a constant state of evolution. Many of its members still look enviously at the powers of the Scottish Parliament and would like to see the assembly become a parliament, while other AMs fail to see the need for extending the assembly's powers any further. As part of the coalition agreement, however, the Welsh Liberal Democrats were able to have a commission set up to consider the future role and powers of the Welsh Assembly. By the end of the assembly's second term, it was clear that the institution had brought a number of benefits to the Welsh nation (see Box 8.4).

The Richard Commission was run by a senior Labour peer, Lord Richard of Ammanford, who was appointed the chair in July 2002.

Box 8.4 The benefits of Welsh devolution

In the first two terms of the Welsh Assembly, it became apparent that a number of benefits had accrued from devolution in Wales.

1. The National Assembly has given Wales a much stronger sense of identity and importance on the national and international scenes. The First Minister has become the recognised face of the Welsh nation in Britain and abroad.
2. The assembly is much more open and accessible than the old Welsh Office. Much of the working of government, and the assembly itself, are open to public view.
3. Devolution has brought the government closer to the people and made it more responsive to local communities on issues such as the closure of hospitals and post offices.
4. Opinion polls show that the Welsh public is now firmly in favour of devolution. Polls from 2003 onwards showed that now only around 20 per cent of the Welsh population would like no devolution. In the 1997 assembly referendum it was around 50 per cent.
5. The National Assembly Government has been keen to establish its own Welsh policies. In part these are centred around the concept of 'localism'. This means that local communities have more influence over the way that services are delivered than elsewhere in the United Kingdom.

6. Those policies in devolved subjects are now drawn up with reference to circumstances and needs in Wales – previously the Welsh Office served to put a Welsh spin (of varying strength) on initiatives/policies which were drawn up to address issues in England, and may not have been so relevant to Wales.

7. All the British political parties have developed separate policies from their constituent bodies in England. Labour, for example, has created its so-called 'clear red water' to distinguish it from New Labour in London.

8. Devolution has increased accountability of Welsh quangos (ASPBs) by integrating them directly into the Welsh Assembly.

9. Secondary legislation now undergoes a more detailed examination than under the old Welsh Office. This has removed a democratic deficit of the previous system of governance in Wales.

10. The government of Wales is now run by people elected by the Welsh electorate rather than under the old Welsh Office system whereby the Secretary of State, often an English MP, was selected by the British government. This has removed a another democratic deficit.

11. It has kept in Cardiff, talented politicians and civil servants who would previously have developed their careers in London. This, in turn, has been beneficial to the Welsh economy and to the social development of the nation.

12. It has increased employment. The assembly government has been able to transfer civil-service posts in order to boost job prospects in traditionally high unemployment areas such as Merthyr Tydfil.

When the commission reported back in April 2004 it recommended that, by the year 2011 or sooner if possible, the assembly:

1. should have its delegated powers enhanced;
2. should be given primary law-making powers;
3. should increase its membership from sixty to eighty and that all should be elected by STV;
4. should be reconstituted with a separate legislature and executive.

There was one major problem with the Richard Commission's recommendations, as the pro-devolutionists discovered. It had reported back eleven months after the most pro-devolutionary party, the Welsh Liberal Democrats, had left the coalition government. For the first two years, the post-May 2003 assembly saw Labour with exactly half the seats in the Welsh Assembly. As the other political parties could not form a coalition government between them, it left Labour in charge of the assembly government. The Wales Labour Party, which is traditionally of a 'conservative' nature in respect to devolution and contains many elements, particularly from local government and Westminster, who were openly hostile towards increasing the assembly's powers, rejected Richard's recommendation of primary law-making powers and an STV system by '2 to 1' in their internal consultation exercise. This was then endorsed by the Wales Labour Party's special conference on 12 September 2004.

Rhodri Morgan, Wales First Minster, and Peter Hain, the Secretary of State for Wales, now saw the progress of the Richard Commission through an obscure chapter subsection 13.2 (called 13.2 plus) within the report. This allows for a framework-type legislation to be passed through the Houses of Parliament without any scrutiny. Those outside the Labour Party, including academics, lawyers, and members of the Richard Commission, the Electoral Commission and the House of Lords, described the plan as unworkable.

Better Governance for Wales, the Wales Labour policy document produced in 2004, made it clear there would be no primary law-making powers for the assembly in the foreseeable future. In both assembly elections, Labour had gained only one AMS seat in 1999, and none in 2003. Many in the party had always been hostile to proportional representation and deeply resented the present AMS system and its members who composed all but ten of the opposition's membership of thirty. With the evidence gathered by the Richard Commission and by other academic bodies, it became apparent that the Welsh Assembly had a number of drawbacks, not all of which could be sorted out through its own recommendations (see Box 8.5).

The Government of Wales Act 2006: a Welsh parliament at last?

The Government of Wales Act 2006 makes two important changes that will make the Welsh Assembly more like a Welsh parliament.

1. Splitting the executive from the legislature
The Government of Wales Act 1998 made the Welsh Assembly a corporate body. This meant that there was no separation of the

Box 8.5 The drawbacks of Welsh devolution

In its first two terms of office between 1999 and 2007, the Welsh Assembly suffered from a number of drawbacks, some of which will be rectified by the Government of Wales Act 2006. The foremost of these are:

1. Much of the Welsh Assembly's period of existence has been dominated by a Labour administration. The Labour Party in Wales is not pluralist in nature and does not co-operate well with other political parties. This has not resulted, therefore, in an era of consensus politics that many thought would occur.

2. There is little (public or) media interest in the Welsh Assembly – partly because there are no national Welsh media to speak of. There are no Welsh national daily newspapers apart from the *Western Mail*, and about 35 per cent of households in Wales are tuned to English-based transmitters. The British media take no interest in the Assembly so its proceedings (plenary and committee) are rarely available to the Welsh people who are often not aware of what the Assembly does – nor what it has done. (Its proceedings are rarely covered and therefore it is surrounded by widespread public ambivalence.)

3. The assimilation of Welsh quangos into Welsh government and the expansion of Welsh Assembly government civil service numbers have led to accusations of a period of 'big government' or 'state-centred society'.

4. The committee system, designed to hold the government to account has proved inadequate to do so. This is partially because of the inadequate scrutiny abilities of many Assembly members. The Assembly was established as a corporate body and there is no clear divide between the legislature and the executive.

5. As **primary law-making powers** have been retained by the Westminster parliament, the Assembly has little opportunity to make real change even in areas where it has 'devolved' responsibility.

6. Most of the secondary legislation made by the Assembly concerns points of detail – not very exciting or interesting – which does not attract attention from the media nor able politicians.

7. There have been too few Welsh Assembly members to provide a large enough pool from which to draw government ministers or to scrutinise properly the government over all issues.

8. The quality and calibre of Assembly Members have sometimes been much weaker than those selected for Westminster.

This has sometimes led them to referred to as the 'second eleven'.

9. Elections to the Welsh Assembly have become seen as a stepping stone to Westminster by some Assembly Members rather than as an end in itself. This is particularly true of Conservative AMs.

10. The process of allocating legislative powers to the Welsh Assembly and the process of secondary legislation remain complex and confusing.

11. The divide between the powers of the Welsh Assembly and Westminster remains unclear in a number of areas, particularly on matters of law and order. Officials and politicians in Whitehall are as confused as anyone about the devolution settlement for Wales – this means they often devise policies without reference to Wales because (a) they are unaware that it is a non-devolved issue so it is their responsibility and (b) even when they are aware, they do not consider the possible impact of their policy on areas which are non-devolved, for example, the closure of post offices and its impact on the social and community policies of Wales.

12. Little of the Welsh Assembly Government's primary legislative programme has found its way into law through the processes at Westminster.

13. There is still widespread indifference towards the Welsh Assembly, particularly in North Wales.

14. The assembly lacks representation at the heart of the British government in Westminster. The Assembly has an office in Brussels to represent its interests to the European Commission, but not in London, despite the fact that Whitehall departments have non-devolved responsibilities for Wales and responsibility for primary legislation for Wales. The Assembly therefore has to rely on the Wales Office, which is a division within another government department, for its voice in London.

executive from the legislature so that the whole assembly 'exercised its functions on behalf of the Crown'. This was mainly because the assembly was initially planned to be based on the old local government model of being run by committees. Even when the first Government of Wales Bill was going through parliament, however, parliament had decided that the assembly should be run on a cabinet system rather than by committee. Once this decision had been made and, in conjunction with the desire of many of the newly elected AMs to feel and behave like parliamentarians, it was inevitable that the Welsh Assembly would try to become more like a parliament.

In February 2002 when the assembly debated its own *Review of Procedure*, it approved unanimously a motion calling for 'the clearest possible separation of powers between the Government and the Assembly'. From March of that year, the ministers and civil servants who exercise the executive powers on behalf of the assembly have called themselves the 'Welsh Assembly Government'. The wider assembly and their supporting services have gone by the title 'Assembly Parliamentary Service'.

The Government of Wales Act 2006, which followed on from the 2005 Wales Office's White Paper *Better Governance for Wales*, formally acknowledged what has been occurring since 2002 by establishing a Welsh Assembly Government as a separate entity, but accountable to the Welsh Assembly. The First Minister is now appointed by the Queen after nomination by the Welsh Assembly. The assembly appoints up to twelve ministers and deputy Ministers 'upon her approval'. These ministers then act on behalf of the Crown rather than on that of the assembly. They are supported in their task by a Counsel General who provides legal advice to the cabinet.

Box 8.6 The Welsh Assembly's new role

Ministers are directly accountable to the assembly for the exercise of their powers. If they lose a no confident vote, they have to resign. Ministers, however, no longer have to attend committees but the assembly has much more power to determine its own committee structure than it did prior to 2006. The assembly has the power to block the Welsh Assembly Government's budget by refusing to 'vote' down the money needed to finance the budget. It is also able to make the appointments to the offices of the Auditor General for Wales and the Public Services Ombudsman for Wales which scrutinise the government's operation of public services.

The assembly has its own support service provided under the Presiding Officer, Deputy Presiding Officer and Clerk to the Assembly. The role of this support and its nature are determined by a body called the Assembly Commission made up from the assembly's Presiding Officer and AMs from the four largest political parties.

It is the assembly ministers who are responsible for most of the policy-determination and law-making undertaken by the assembly. At the same time, these order-making powers have to be ratified by the assembly.

2. Enhanced legislative powers for the Welsh Assembly
The Government of Wales Act 2006 increases the assembly's legislative powers, potentially in three stages.

Stage 1 Framework legislation is enacted by conferring wider powers on the assembly to make subordinate legislation. This means that all Westminster legislation which goes into those areas controlled by the assembly is now drafted in order to allow the assembly 'maximum freedom of manoeuvre' in Wales in delivering policy.

Stage 2 Orders in Council These allow parliament to confer enhanced legislative powers on the assembly in relation to specified subject matter within devolved fields. An Order in Council enables the assembly to pass its own legislation within the scope of its powers delegated by parliament. Orders in Council are not normally scrutinised by MPs in Westminster, but the Government of Wales Act 2006 allows them to do so. At the same time, these orders are scrutinised by the assembly in Wales – resulting in 'double scrutiny'. This type of legislation is known as Assembly Measures.

Stage 3 Primary legislative powers These will be granted following a referendum. If the result is successful, the assembly will be allowed 'to make law on all the matters within its devolved fields of competence without further recourse to Parliament'. There are 'constitutional locks' on getting a referendum. Such a referendum would not occur before 2011 (the date of the assembly's fourth term in office). In 2006 the Welsh Secretary, Peter Hain, indicated that, under a Labour Westminster government, this would not occur before 2016.

In the event of a 'yes' vote in any referendum, Westminster would continue to be able to legislate for Wales. This would mean that procedures similar to the Sewel motions that regulate the relationship between the Westminster and the Scottish parliaments would be used. It means that, if the Welsh Assembly agrees the legislation passed for England, it would at the same time apply to Wales without

Box 8.7 Controversy surrounds changing the Welsh Assembly's electoral system

The Richard Commission recommended that the Welsh Assembly adopt a system of STV for an eighty-member assembly. The Wales Labour Party was also determined to change the electoral system of the assembly, but not to STV. Instead, it altered the existing system of AMS, in which a candidate could stand in a constituency and on the regional list, to one in which he/she had to stand for one or the other. Labour's reasoning was that its party members and, they claimed, the wider public did not like an electoral system in which people could lose in the constituency but reappear in the assembly as a winning list member. They cited the example of the Clwyd West constituency which, in the 2003 assembly election, had produced a Labour constituency winner yet the three losing opposition members all then came to the assembly through the list system.

Professor Robert Hazell, head of University College, London's Constitution Unit, stated that the change was 'nasty, parochial and seemingly driven by partisan motives'. It was also noted by the Campaign for a Welsh Parliament that Labour did not have any list AMs, while the opposition had twenty. This measure was aimed, therefore, at undermining them. There were similar condemnations from all the opposition political parties in Wales, the Electoral Commission, Institute of Welsh Affairs, Institute of Welsh Politics, and the wider academic community. Those opposing the change to the electoral system pointed to the fact that Wales would now be the only nation in the world operating AMS which barred candidates from standing in the constituency and on the list.

the assembly needing to legislate there as well. This is because the Westminster parliament remains the sovereign in Britain parliament.

The Welsh language

When the social scientist Jonathan Scourfield, looked at Wales and Welshness in a study of Welsh children, one of them commented that 'Mae gormod o bobl siarad Seasneg' (too many people speak English). Across the world English has become one the dominant languages so, in England's immediate neighbour, perhaps the question should be 'how does Welsh survive at all?' The answer, surprisingly, is 'very well considering', The 2001 census revealed that some 28.4 per cent of Wales's populations, or 797,709 out of 2.8 million people, had some knowledge of Welsh. This was a slight improvement on the 1991 census which showed that the language was no longer in decline. The number of those with a knowledge of Welsh was not evenly spread across Wales, however. The proportion of those with a knowledge of Welsh decreases the further one travels from the border between England and Wales. The status of the Welsh language is a political hot potato in Wales. Plaid Cymru was founded mainly around the issues of protecting it and enhancing its status. From the 1960s onwards, a series of civil protests by Cymdeithas yr Iaith Gymraeg (Welsh Language Society), together with pressure from other parties, brought the issue of the Welsh language to the forefront of government policy in Wales.

In 1967 the Welsh Office introduced the first Welsh Language Act which, for the first time, gave the Welsh language equal status to English. Over the ensuing decades the Welsh language was seen more and more as an important political issue. The Conservative Party, which had traditionally been against promoting any issue that encouraged Welsh nationalism, poured millions of pounds into its promotion. After much controversy, it even introduced a Welsh-language television channel, Sianel Pedwar Cymru (Wales Channel Four). In 1988 Welsh was made a compulsory subject for all schoolchildren as part of the National Curriculum in Wales. Then, in 1993, a second Welsh Language Act strengthened the position of Welsh in public life. It established a Welsh Language Board which was responsible for promoting the use of the language and ensuring that public bodies treated the Welsh and English languages equally. The preparations of the Welsh Assembly also saw the issue of the Welsh language brought to the fore, with the equal status of Welsh fundamental to many of the procedures and processes. The assembly is truly bilingual with simultaneous translation of oral proceedings and documentation produced in both languages.

Not everyone was happy with the policies made to promote the Welsh language, however. In the counties where only a small percentage of the population spoke Welsh, there was continued resistance to having to learn Welsh at school and to watching the Welsh Channel Four instead of the English/Scottish television. Various

Welsh public institutions, such as the University of Wales, complained that they could not afford to implement the requirements of the 1993 Welsh Language Act. After their general election defeat in 1997, the Conservatives also came out strongly against the compulsory elements of the Welsh-language legislation. Through their 1999 assembly manifesto, they sought to make Welsh no longer compulsory in post-fourteen education. Yet, despite these protests, the existence of the Welsh language remains important in Welsh life.

Welshness (Cymreictod) and cultural distinctiveness

Under the entry 'For Wales', in the *Encyclopedia Britannica* in the nineteenth century, it stated simply 'see England'. By the late Victorian period, however, with the pressure in part put forward by the rising Welsh Liberal Nationalists, such as David Lloyd George and Tom Ellis, and their desire through the movement Cymru Fydd (Wales to be) to bind politics and Welsh culture in one movement, there arose a Welsh National Party (within the Welsh Liberal Party) which sought to distinguish Wales from England. From then on, Welsh national identity and culture became a political issue of varying importance.

Today, those leading cultural bodies, institutions and figures that are in and surround the Welsh Assembly are said to be the driving force of what is described as Welsh 'civil society'. It is this civil society that was in part responsible for the establishment of the Welsh Assembly which was itself partly the result of the aspirations of a Welsh population who believed their cultural values and norms were different enough to require a separate legislative and executive body to help maintain them.

Threats to Welsh cultural identity

The Welsh economy has been in steady decline for decades. Large areas of Wales have a **GDP** of 67 per cent of the British average. This has meant that Wales has, for the most part, become an area of low-paying jobs but, at the same time, one that attracts inward migrants owing to the lower cost of living, mainly in the price of houses.

Immigration When asked what defines Welsh identity 'being born in Wales' is regarded as being the most important (see Box 8.5).

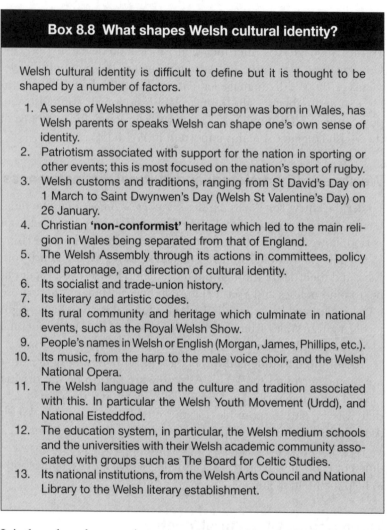

Box 8.8 What shapes Welsh cultural identity?

Welsh cultural identity is difficult to define but it is thought to be shaped by a number of factors.

1. A sense of Welshness: whether a person was born in Wales, has Welsh parents or speaks Welsh can shape one's own sense of identity.
2. Patriotism associated with support for the nation in sporting or other events; this is most focused on the nation's sport of rugby.
3. Welsh customs and traditions, ranging from St David's Day on 1 March to Saint Dwynwen's Day (Welsh St Valentine's Day) on 26 January.
4. Christian **'non-conformist'** heritage which led to the main religion in Wales being separated from that of England.
5. The Welsh Assembly through its actions in committees, policy and patronage, and direction of cultural identity.
6. Its socialist and trade-union history.
7. Its literary and artistic codes.
8. Its rural community and heritage which culminate in national events, such as the Royal Welsh Show.
9. People's names in Welsh or English (Morgan, James, Phillips, etc.).
10. Its music, from the harp to the male voice choir, and the Welsh National Opera.
11. The Welsh language and the culture and tradition associated with this. In particular the Welsh Youth Movement (Urdd), and National Eisteddfod.
12. The education system, in particular, the Welsh medium schools and the universities with their Welsh academic community associated with groups such as The Board for Celtic Studies.
13. Its national institutions, from the Welsh Arts Council and National Library to the Welsh literary establishment.

It is thought to be more important than speaking the Welsh language, living in Wales, or even having Welsh parents. Therefore, the influx of those people not born in Wales is seen by some as a threat to national identity.

Inward migration in some Welsh counties, such as Flintshire, represents almost half the resident population (49 per cent). This dilutes the resident Welsh population. The problem of solely English-speaking people moving into predominantly Welsh-speaking areas is a particularly sensitive political issue. In 2001 a pressure group, Cymuned (Community), began to lobby the Welsh Assembly on issues relating to inward migration and the need to prioritise local housing for local people. In some Welsh-speaking areas, such as Ceredigion, the average property price had by 2005 risen to seven times the average county wage. House prices rises, such as these, prevent many young people from living where they were born and brought up.

Emigration The loss of Welsh graduates and other young Welsh people in search of better-paid jobs to England or to other countries is significant while the overall population remains fairly constant but increasingly ageing. This means that the younger, more educated Welsh people are moving out at the same time as an ageing population is coming to Wales to retire.

Media and the dominance of 'English' values In many parts of Wales neither the Welsh press nor broadcast media are dominant. The main Welsh daily newspaper, the *Western Mail*, is read by only about 10 per cent of the population, while the majority reads the London press. At the same time, the populations of the border, south-eastern and North-eastern counties predominantly receive the English BBC and commercial stations which means that Welsh news and cultural values are not provided to significant numbers of the population.

Dominance of the Westminster parliament Despite the existence of the Welsh Assembly, many in the Westminster parliament, including Labour and Conservative MPs, are nervous about promoting Welsh values that could lead to demands for independence for wales. Therefore, issues such as the assembly's request since its inception for a national holiday to be declared for 1 March, St David's Day, have been rejected.

Conclusion

Since it inception, the National Assembly for Wales has gone through a steady period of evolution. Designed initially more on a local government model of one body being run by a series of committees, in reality, almost from its first day, it sought to become more of a parliament. It soon became known as the Welsh Assembly rather than by its more formal title. The names of First and Cabinet 'Secretaries' were dropped to be replaced by the terms First and Cabinet 'Ministers'. An official opposition developed and the Welsh Assembly Government became separated from the wider Welsh Assembly. From 2007, Welsh government has had its own form of primary law making powers via Westminster through a process known as 'Orders in Council'. In time this may develop, after a referendum in Wales, to primary law-making power coming directly from Cardiff without the need to go through Westminster.

The Welsh Assembly has not been without its problems. It first leader, Alun Michael, was removed in a vote of no confidence. Its new home upon the Cardiff Bay waterfront was five years late in coming and more than fives times costlier than was initially planned. Its development of the NHS in Wales led to much longer waiting lists for operations than was the case across the border in England. Later, the planned merger of many ASPBs into the Welsh Assembly Government was rejected in some parts by the opposition. Nevertheless, over its first two terms, the Welsh Assembly Government was able to develop policy and legislation in Wales that marked it out from its neighbour, England.

While these events were going on, the Welsh language continued to be an integral part of Welsh politics and, at the same time, the cultural distinctiveness of Wales was being in part enhanced, and supported, by the Welsh Assembly. After the government of Wales Act 2006, the Welsh Assembly is now going through another period of evolution.

•••

✓ What you should have learnt from reading this chapter

- When the Welsh Assembly was established, it was thought that it would herald a new era of consensus politics. This period did not last for more than a few months and, in the new period of conflict politics, the First Secretary, Alun Michael, was removed.

- Under Rhodri Morgan, the assembly evolved through periods of coalition with the Welsh Liberal Democrats and later as a minority government.

- The construction of the new Welsh Assembly building caused controversy in its overspend and in its delay.

- The Welsh ASPBs are being integrated into the Welsh Assembly

Government. This process has not been without controversy and some resistance.

- The coalition government established the Richard Commission to examine the future of the Welsh Assembly. The commission recommended an eighty-member assembly elected by STV with primary law-making powers.

- Under a Labour administration, the Welsh Assembly Government rejected the main Richard Commission proposals and instead brought forward its own more limited changes which would separate the Welsh legislature from the executive and allow for some primary legislative powers through Westminster.

- The Welsh language is important in distinguishing Welsh culture and politics from that of other nations.

- The Government of Wales Act 2006 has altered the Welsh Assembly so that it is more like a legislative parliament, with a divide being clearly made between the executive and legislature.

Glossary of key terms

ASPB Assembly-sponsored public bodies (quangos).
ESRC Economic and Social Research Council.
Framework legislation An act which just provides the outline of what it wishes to undertake, with the detail to be filled in by secondary legislation.
GDP Gross domestic product, an economic measure of the wealth of an area.
Non-conformist A Christian who worships through the Methodist, Baptist or other movements but not through the Anglican or Roman Catholic Churches.
Primary law-making powers The ability to make and determine law-making powers without recourse to another legislative body. For Wales these law-making powers would mean that laws (acts) would be made in Cardiff instead of at Westminster.

Likely examination questions

Critically evaluate the view that the Welsh language is the only real difference between Welsh and English culture.

To what extent is it true to say that the Welsh Assembly Government's policy programme ran smoothly during its first and second terms in office?

The proposal concerning tax raising powers for the Welsh Assembly was left out of the Richard Commission report. Do you think that the Welsh Assembly should be able to raise its own taxes?

Helpful websites

www.richardcommission.gov.uk The Richard Commission's website contains a great deal of information on the development of the assembly and on the potential for its future.

The other relevant web sites are shown in Chapter 7.

Suggestion for further reading

J. Morris, *Wales, Epic Views of a Small Country*, Penguin, 2000.

J. Scourfield, A. Davies and S. Holland, 'Wales and Welshness in Middle Childhood' in *Contemporary Wales*, Vol. 16, University of Wales Press, 2003.

G. Talfan Davies and J. Osmond, 'Culture and Indentity' in *Birth of Welsh Democracy: The First Term of the National Assembly for Wales*, eds John Osmond and J. Barry Jones, Institute of Welsh Affairs, 2003.

B. Taylor and K. Thomson (eds), *Scotland and Wales: Nations Again?* University of Wales Press, 1999.

C. Williams, 'Passports to Wales? Race, Nation and Indentity' in B. Taylor and K. Thomson (eds), *Scotland and Wales: Nations Again?* University of Wales Press, 1999.

CHAPTER 9

Northern Ireland: Historical Political Development

Contents

Overview

A nineteenth-century proverb says 'happy is a country with no history'. Nowhere is this more true or important than in Northern Ireland. Events happening centuries ago still affect and influence the lives of people there today and the religious divide between Protestants and Roman Catholics remains as acute as almost anywhere else in Europe. Long before 'ethnic cleansing' became synonymous with events in the former Yugoslavia, it was occurring in Belfast and across the rest of Ireland as the mixed communities of Protestants and Catholics were being broken up and segregated. Over three centuries, events in Ireland often came to dominate British governments' domestic political agendas. Therefore, it is possible to examine contemporary political events in Northern Ireland only after first knowing something of its historical development. This chapter briefly examines the historical events that have shaped the political situation in Northern Ireland over the last 500 years. The importance of the religious divide between Roman Catholics and Protestants is examined. The development of Irish Home Rule, the Irish civil war and the establishment of the Stormont Parliament, with its subsequent failure, are detailed. The division in politics between nationalists and unionists, their subsequent development and the development of the peace process are also examined.

Key issues to be covered in this chapter

- Irish history from the arrival of the Roman Catholic Church to the Act of Union
- The importance and relevance of the 1801 Act of Union
- How religion is at the heart of the problems in Northern Ireland
- The Victorian era, and the modern development of Irish nationalism
- The background to the Orange Order and politicisation of the Unionist cause
- The 1920 Government of Ireland Act and the 1922 Treaty of Ireland
- The role and functions of the Northern Ireland Parliament (Stormont)
- The development of Northern Ireland into a Protestant state
- The road to a peaceful solution to Northern Ireland's troubles

The long history of a troubled nation

The island of Ireland is not only physically separated from the other nations of the United Kingdom but, since 1922, it has also been split into two separate nations, Southern Ireland (Eire), an independent nation, and Northern Ireland (Ulster), a province of the United Kingdom. For much of the last five hundred years Ireland has been the most troubled of all of the nations that make up the British Isles. Famine, rebellion, emigration and war have continually shaped and reshaped the island.

Owing to the fact that attempts to deal with devolutionary pressures in Ireland dominated the later part of nineteenth-century British politics, the whole concept of the 'devolution of powers' has its origins in the Home Rule for Ireland Movement. Subsequently, the first example of a devolved parliament in the United Kingdom was that of Stormont in Northern Ireland.

The thousand troubled years of history

The Romans never conquered Ireland but, ironically, it was to become the part of the British Isles most dominated by Rome's greatest legacy, the Roman **Catholic** Church. For many centuries, Irish missionaries went out to convert the rest of Europe, and one, St David, became the patron saint of Wales. By AD 800, Ireland comprised a series of individual kingdoms. It was the Vikings who settled in Ireland and established towns, of which Dublin became the chief one. From the twelfth century on, through conquest and intermarriage with the Irish nobility, the English controlled about two-thirds of Ireland. By the fifteenth century, however, **direct rule** by an English monarch had been reduced to Dublin and its hinterland.

Despite England's loss of direct control, Irish independence was halted by Poynings's Law of 1494, when the Lord Deputy, Sir Edward Poynings, ruled that the English Privy Council must approve the summoning of an Irish parliament and any legislation of that parliament. This law was to remain in place from that time, and any moves towards independence or against English rule were ruthlessly crushed. In 1534 Henry VIII broke the rebellion of Thomas Fitzgerald, and the English king smashed the power of Kildare and the Geraldines, taking Ireland under direct rule and dividing the country into shires after the English model. In 1541 Henry became the first English king to be known as 'King' rather than 'Lord' of Ireland and, at the same time, made himself the head of the Church in Ireland.

Over the following centuries a process of colonisation occurred across Ireland. The government of Kings James I and James II intensified the policy of imposing **Protestant** settlers on Catholic areas in what were known as 'plantations'. For the next few centuries, there were frequent rebellions by the Catholics which were suppressed by Protestants.

The Treaty of Limerick, 1691, promised religious freedom for Roman Catholics but the promise was never honoured, and there was, instead, a series of anti-Catholic laws. Catholics were excluded from the Irish parliament in 1692 and disenfranchised in 1727. In 1781, however, anti-Catholic laws were relaxed and Poynings's Law was repealed in 1782, creating a de facto parliamentary independence. The 'Irish problem' continued to exist and therefore, as a solution, Prime Minister William Pitt proposed to unite the Irish and Westminster parliaments. Although initially resisted by the Protestants, the Act of Union was passed in 1800, coming into force on 1 January 1801. Article 1 of the Union with Ireland Act 1800 stated that the United Kingdoms of Great Britain and Ireland would, from 1 January 1801, and 'for ever after, be united into one kingdom, by the name of the United Kingdom of Great Britain and Ireland'.

For the next 120 years the Act of Union remained unaltered. The act allowed for the continued prosperity of the ruling classes in the ever-expanding British Empire. Irish public administration continued to be run in Dublin under the Lord Lieutenant and the Chief Secretary for Ireland who was a cabinet minister. As in Scotland, Ireland also had a judiciary of its own but no independent legislature. From now until its independence, Ireland would be a subordinate country ruled by the British and its allies rather than an integrated part of England, as Wales was.

Ireland in the Victorian era

During Queen Victoria's reign, Irish nationalism continued to develop. An upper-class Catholic lawyer, called Daniel O'Connell, formed the Catholic Association in order to bring pressure to bear on the government by such means as electing Roman Catholic MPs. Two years later the association was dissolved by the government which then sought to suppress it. In 1828 O'Connell himself was elected as MP for County Clare but, as a Catholic was unable to take his seat. Catholic emancipation occurred the following year. The attention of the people then turned from religion towards social and economic questions, especially regarding land tenure (tenant farmers). As unrest grew, agitation for repeal of the Act of Union resumed after 1829. O'Connell founded the National Repeal Association in 1841. For the next eighty years various groups, ranging from the Young Ireland Movement to the Home Rule Association, campaigned unsuccessfully to have the 'hated' Act of Union repealed.

The defining event of the nineteenth century in Ireland, was the potato famine (the Great Famine) of the 1840s. There was little industry in Ireland, and the majority of the population was based on the land. The overreliance of the Irish on potatoes was in part due to Irish inheritance laws, which continually divided into smaller plots, land and partly because of a lack of tenants' rights for most farmers. The problems in agriculture meant that, when the potato harvest failed over a number of years, about a million people died in Ireland and three million emigrated to Britain, many to Wales and Scotland, a million of whom went on to the United States. In the space of a few years, Ireland had lost almost half its population.

Many American Irish, including those who had fought in the American civil war, supported a secret society called the Irish Republican Brotherhood (IRB), better known as **Fenians**. In time, the IRB would promote rebellion against the British across Ireland. Though Irish nationalism was associated with the Catholics, it was an Anglo-Irish Protestant, Charles Parnell, MP for Meath, who formed a group known as the New Departure which went beyond the more passive Irish Home Rule Movement. Its MPs were disruptive in parliament and caused increasing problems for Liberal Prime Minister, William Ewart Gladstone. In the 1885 election eighty-six Irish nationalist MPs were returned while the number of Liberal MPs was so reduced that Gladstone could form a government only with the assistance of Irish members. Parnell used a combination of the Irish party's strength in parliament, together with this Liberal alliance, to persuade Gladstone that Ireland had spoken and to accept the necessity of Irish Home Rule – a bill to bring it about was placed before parliament in 1886. This move brought out the full hostility of the Conservatives, Ulster Protestants and a significant number of Liberal MPs, led by Joseph Chamberlain, to Home Rule. Home Rule was defeated; Chamberlain's dissident Liberals became Liberal Unionists, and left the Liberals to joined up with the Conservatives. The Liberal administration collapsed, replaced by a pro-union Conservative-Liberal Unionist government which opposed any Home Rule for Ireland bill and would block its arrival in either the House of Commons or House of Lords until after World War I. In the light of the failure of Home Rule, Parnell's career went into decline and the Irish party's fortunes declined with it. In 1900, at the general election, the Irish Parliamentary Party made something of a comeback under the leadership of John Redmond but the younger and more radical elements were now backing the more extreme position advocated by the political group known as Sinn Fein (Ourselves Alone).

For the Irish nationalists, Redmond's main hope came after 1910 with Herbert Asquith's Liberal government but, even with the Liberals, they were still unable to get a Home Rule bill past the Conservative-controlled House of Lords before war broke out in 1914. Redmond supported Irish involvement in the war, something which cost him his popularity which decreased as the war itself became unpopular. When the Irish Republican Brotherhood and Sinn Fein promoted the Dublin Easter Rising in 1916 Redmond failed to condemn the harsh treatment by the British of the republican leaders. The threat of bringing conscription to the Irish in 1918 also added more fuel to the nationalist fire. After the war, Sinn Fein, led by Eamon de Valera, won seventy-three seats compared to just six for Redmond's Home Rule Party. The Irish Unionist Party won twenty-six seats, mostly in Ulster. The seventy-three Sinn Fein MPs refused to go to Westminster and, instead, sat in their own parliament in Dáil Éireann in Dublin. Although it first met on 21 January 1919, it had no powers. On the same day that the Dáil Éireann met, the newly formed Irish Republican Army (IRA) shot dead two Irish policemen in County Tipperary, marking the start of what became, known as the 'Irish War of Independence'.

The Unionists become politicised

In 1905 the Ulster Unionist Council (UUC) was formed. It was linked with the Conservative Party and would evolve to become the Ulster Unionist Party and dominate Irish politics for nearly a century. In 1911 (Sir) Edward Carson, a noted Dublin lawyer, became leader of the UUC. Carson then set about galvanising the Protestants of Ireland against Home Rule, often bringing together rallies of tens of thousands of supporters. Unionists wanted to remain governed by a Protestant London and not a Roman Catholic Dublin. To confirm this viewpoint, in January 1912 the Ulster Volunteer Force (UVF) was formed by militarily experienced gentry to support the Unionist cause.

Box 9.1 The Orange Order

While some Protestants and Roman Catholics joined together to seek Home Rule for Ireland, another group of Protestants was seeking to make its own claims for Ireland's future. This was the Orange Order, a solely Protestant organisation, founded in County Armagh in 1795 as a counterweight to the 'Defenders', a Roman Catholic secret society. It was also in part a restoration of the Orange Institution which had supported William (III) of Orange in 1688. William's victory over the Catholic James II, at the Battle of the Boyne in 1690, was, from 1796, celebrated annually in parades by Protestants. The Orange Order soon spread across Irish counties and was to form the core of 'loyalists' whenever British rule in Ireland was challenged. Despite their 'loyalty', the Orange Order was increasingly seen as a threat to the Union, as a disorderly ally causing severe sectarian rioting in Belfast leading to hundreds of death. In 1825, and again between 1832 and 1844, it was banned. In the nineteenth and twentieth centuries, the Orange Order dominated politics in Northern Ireland, as it sought to ensure that the North remained a dominantly Protestant state with Catholics sidelined. The order was powerful enough to bring the country to a halt if matters did not go its way.

The Orange Order is still a central part of Protestant life in Northern Ireland today, and, with their system of lodges, the Orange societies are organised in a similar way to Freemasons. It enjoys close ties with the Unionist parties and celebrates this history through public parades during what is called the 'marching season'.

Before trouble could arise, Britain was plunged into World War I. The opposition in Ulster from Edward Carson and the Orange Order to Home Rule and a mutiny by British army officers at the Curragh Camp meant that implementation of Home Rule was shelved until after the end of the war. Carson had already gained the concession that the six counties of Ulster would be able in any settlement to delay joining the devolved Irish parliament for six years.

The Treaty of Ireland, 1922

In 1920, while this conflict was going on, the government passed the Government of Ireland Act. The act gave Ireland two parliaments (each with a prime minister), one for the North and one for the South, both accountable to Westminster. The first elections for the Northern Ireland parliament were held in May 1921 and the Unionists gained forty of the fifty-two seats. The parliament first met in Belfast in June 1921 with the new Prime Minister being the Ulster Unionist leader, Sir James Craig. This new deal was a disaster for all Irish nationalists who wanted to united Ireland, and a victory for those who did not.

Elections were also held for the nationalist parliament in Dublin in May 1921, and Sinn Fein took 124 seats, with the remaining four going to Unionist candidates. Sinn Fein refused to recognise the parliament, however, and instead continued to meet in Dáil Éireann. Only the four Unionists attended the new parliament. Under their leader, Michael Collins, the IRA continued to fight on for more independence but a stalemate ensued and a truce was signed between the IRA and the British on 11 July 1921. Some four months later a treaty was hammered out between Michael Collins on behalf of the IRA and Lloyd George for the British government. Collins, however, failed fully to consult his colleagues and they ejected many of those who rejected partition. This, in turn, led to Collins's assassination a short time later.

The 'Anglo-Irish Treaty', which was agreed between Collins and the British government, replaced the Dublin Home-Rule parliament, created by the Government of Ireland Act 1920, with a much more independent parliament. The new country was to be called the 'Irish Free State' and had its own army but remained within the British Commonwealth. With Michael Collins dead, it was the Sinn Fein leader, Eamon de Valera, who became the first Prime Minister of the Irish Free State. The United Kingdom was renamed 'The United Kingdom of Great Britain and Northern Ireland' to reflect the change.

In 1922 the Protestant establishment, led by their new parliament and prime minister at Stormont, used the excuse of the violence in the north and the civil war in the south to strengthen their own internal security power. The Civil Authorities (Special Powers) Act 1922 gave widespread powers of detention and internment to the authorities. It allowed the security forces in Northern Ireland to 'arrest without warrants, detain without trial, search homes without warrants, prohibit meetings and processions, and hang and whip offenders'. The Ulster Special Constabulary was also founded in 1922. It was a paramilitary, part-time police force in the mould of the infamous 'Black and Tans' and recruited largely from the ranks of the Ulster Volunteer Force. Known as the B Specials, they were notorious for their discriminatory use of violence in support of Protestantism.

The Protestant state takes shape

Between 1922 and 1972, the Protestant state of Northern Ireland was maintained jointly by the Anglo-Irish, Church of Ireland establishment and a largely Presbyterian working-class rank-and-file organised within the lodges of the Orange Order. The Catholic population of Northern Ireland was excluded from any real power, and their middle class became increasingly resentful.

In 1963 a liberal Unionist Ulster Prime Minister, Terence O'Neill, began to make modest reforms, admittedly under some pressure from London. At about the same time, owing to the events that were unfolding in the United States, a great deal of international interest and involvement had been stirred up by Martin Luther King's campaign to gain civil rights for the black community. In 1966, the Northern Ireland Civil Rights Association (NICRA) was founded in County Derry and immediately declared that its aim was to gain the right of 'one man, one vote' in local elections, extending the franchise to the whole adult population and getting rid of a business vote that gave some people a right to as many as six votes! In 1968, a peaceful march in Derry was broken up mainly by police overreaction and brutality. Most of the marchers, together with the founders of the

Social Democratic and Labour Party (SDLP), Gerry Fitt and John Hume, were advocates of peaceful protest. A republican element in the movement, however, wanted direct action.

There was a Protestant counter-attack against the protest movement, led from within the government by the Minister for Home Affairs, William Craig, who directed heavy-handed police action, and by militant Unionists such as the Reverend Ian Paisley. The latter founded the Protestant Unionist Party which later became the Democratic Unionist Party (DUP). Harold's Wilson's Labour government in Westminster was increasingly split over what to do about the disturbances but ruled out direct intervention for the time being. In November 1968, O'Neill granted a number of reforms that were well received by NICRA but not by Unionists such as Ian Paisley and William Craig. In February 1969, O'Neill called a general election which he duly won but with the Unionist vote seriously split. In April that year he resigned and, in the subsequent by-election, his seat at Stormont was won by Ian Paisley. The sectarian divide had now become almost unbridgeable. A prominent leader of NICRA, John Hume, defeated the Nationalist leader Eddie McAteer. Hume, and other independents elected in 1969, formed the Social and Democratic Labour Party in the following year. For the next two decades, the SDLP would be the main political party for those Catholic or Nationalist supporters who sought a peaceful settlement to Northern Ireland's problems.

From the summer Orange marching season onwards, events in Northern Ireland spiralled out of control to the extent that a Protestant mob, spearheaded by off-duty B Specials, began the **ethnic cleansing** of areas in Belfast of their Catholic residents. This horrified the Wilson government and it put pressure on Ulster Prime Minister, James Chichester-Clark, to make further reforms, including the disbandment of the B Specials and a return to proportional representation in local elections. The British army was also sent in to protect the Catholics. The army was soon playing a key role in supporting the Royal Ulster Constabulary (RUC) which, in turn, reactivated the IRA in the north with a new active faction calling itself the Provisional IRA, known as 'the Provos'. Its political wing was the 'Provisional Sinn Fein'.

The Conservative government under Edward Heath, which came into power in June 1970, made an effort to stay out of Ulster and concentrated on trying to get the IRA out of Catholic areas. In February 1971, Gunner Robert Curtis became the first British soldier to be killed by the provisional IRA, and Northern Ireland Prime Minister, James Chichester-Clark, demanded reinforcements. London, however, did not want to be drawn into the troubles and Chichester-Clark resigned in March to be replaced by Brian Faulkner. Within months, Faulkner invoked the existing emergency powers act to reintroduce internment without trial. Thousands of Catholics were interned in an old American Air Force base, Long Kesh. This resulted merely in pushing many innocent Catholics directly into the arms of the IRA. On 30 January 1972 (Bloody Sunday) paratroopers opened fire on a civil-rights march in Derry, killing thirteen people in circumstances that are still in dispute. This act led to the almost complete collapse of Catholic opposition to political violence. Stormont was thoroughly discredited and the British Prime Minister, Edward Heath, wanted to be rid of it. On 22 March 1972, Stormont was prorogued and, within a week, direct rule came into effect with William Whitelaw as Secretary of State for Northern Ireland.

The British and Irish governments and the road to a peaceful solution to Northern Ireland's troubles

Within a short time, it became apparent that the British government would not be able to defeat the IRA, while the sectarian divide meant that the movement would continue to receive strong Catholic support. Over the coming two decades, thousands in Northern Ireland and beyond would lose their lives. A peaceful solution to the Northern Ireland 'problem' would now be a central part of every British and Irish Prime Ministers political agenda. Over the next three decades, while the military and terrorist campaigns continued, there was a series of attempts to bring Unionists and Nationalists together to end direct rule and achieve a peaceful solution to 'troubles'.

In 1973 the Northern Ireland Constitution Act resulted in the election by the single transferable vote (STV) system of proportional representation of a seventy-eight-seat, multi-party assembly and a power-sharing executive composed of the Official Unionists, the Alliance Party and the SDLP; it took office on 1 January 1974. This was supported by a new settlement agreed at Sunningdale in Berkshire.

Representatives of the IRA took part, and a proposed Council of Ireland made up of seven representatives from Dublin and seven from Belfast was agreed. The Unionists, were on the whole, opposed to the Sunningdale Agreement because of its recognition of the role of Dublin in the government of Northern Ireland. In the February 1974 General Election, eleven of the twelve candidates elected were opposed to the Sunningdale Agreement. The executive was undermined by this and by a general strike called by the Protestant Ulster Workers' Council in May 1974. Brian Faulkner resigned from the executive and as leader of the Unionists. The Northern Ireland Act of 1974, which followed, dissolved the assembly and reimposed direct rule.

Conservative Prime Minister, Margaret Thatcher (who survived an IRA assassination attempt in 1986), did use the political carrot and stick with Northern Ireland. As well as continuing a direct military war against the IRA, her Northern Ireland Secretary, James Prior, began a process of what he called 'rolling devolution' in 1982. A Northern Ireland Assembly of seventy-eight members was elected in October of that year. The Unionists refused to share power with the republicans. Sinn Fein and the SDLP then boycotted the assembly, and the venture was abandoned in June 1986. During this period, however, a step forward was taken in the peace process. An agreement of 1985 between the London and Dublin governments, signed by Margaret Thatcher and Dr Garrett Fitzgerald, and known as the Anglo-Irish or Hillsborough Agreement, was a major advance because Dublin openly recognised for the first time that there could be change in Northern Ireland only with the consent of the majority of people there. Hillsborough allowed for regular meetings between British and Irish ministers and a permanent staff of British and Irish civil servants based at Stormont to help negotiate agreement on cross-border disputes.

On 15 December 1993, John Major and Albert Reynolds set out a Joint Declaration (also known as the Downing Street Declaration). This stated that:

1. the people of Ireland, North and South, should freely determine their future;
2. this could be expressed in new structures arising out of the three-stranded relationship;

3. there could be no change in Northern Ireland's status without freely given majority consent;
4. this majority consent could be withheld;
5. the consent principle should be written into the Irish constitution;
6. Sinn Fein could enter into negotiations once the IRA had renounced violence.

This agreement was now backed not only in Dublin and London but, importantly, by President Clinton in Washington. The Irish voice is particularly strong in American politics owing to the large-scale immigration into the United States. Now both Dublin and London,

---

Box 9.2 Why did it take so long to come to a peaceful solution?

- Mistrust between Unionists and Protestants caused by the fear that one group would dominate the other.
- Religious, historical and cultural factors that kept Catholic and Protestant communities apart and from sharing common causes.
- The geographical isolation of Northern Ireland and its structural economic decline meant that there was not the wide-scale immigration that might have reshaped the culture.
- Intransigence in Southern Ireland. It would not amend its constitution which stated that Northern Ireland was an integral part of Southern Ireland.
- Intransigence in Northern Ireland's Protestant community which did not want any role in the north for the Dublin government.
- The 'hands-off' approach of successive British governments which did not want to interfere in devolved Northern Irish matters.
- British governments' preference for 'loyal' Protestant unionists over 'disloyal' Catholic nationalists.
- Mistrust of the British government by Catholics and later by Unionists Each side feared that it would be 'sold out' to appease the other side.
- Unionist and wider British public pressure on the British government which did not to be seen to be 'appeasing terrorists'.
- The increasing militantancy of politics in the Protestant and in the Catholic camps.

as well as Washington, sought to win agreement for the Declaration, not only in Northern Ireland but also in their own countries.

Soon after his election in 1997, New Labour Prime Minister, Tony Blair, with his Northern Ireland Secretary, Mo Mowlam, made serious efforts to bring the peace process back on track. Both sought to make progress from the Downing Street Declaration. On 15 July the entire province was horrified when 'loyalist' gunmen dragged Roman Catholic Bernadette Martin from her Protestant boyfriend's home and shot her dead. Three days later Gerry Adams and Martin McGuinness for Sinn Fein urged the IRA to call a ceasefire and, on 19 July, that ceasefire was effected. In September, the government accepted that the IRA ceasefire had lasted long enough for Sinn Fein to be admitted to the peace talks and, as a result, Sinn Fein agreed to the decommissioning of weapons (the 'Mitchell Principles' named after a US senator). On Good Friday 1998 the renewed peace talks bore fruit when agreement was reached that there would be a newly elected Northern Ireland Assembly.

Conclusion

Ireland was one of the first colonies that the British developed. The successful struggle for Southern Irish independence was seen as an inspiration across the British Empire for other nationalist movements. After all, if nationalism could succeed in creating independence in the British Isles, then surely others would be able to gain it elsewhere. Yet, well after these other nationalists had won their independence and the sun had set forever on the British Empire, the problems of the colonial legacy in Ireland continued. Northern Ireland represented one the plainest examples of how a religious divide could result in an almost intractable political problem. The Protestant suppression of Catholic rights, in part fuelled by Southern Ireland refusing to give up its own demands that the country should be united, led to a political head of steam building that erupted in the late 1960s. The violence associated with the troubles of Northern Ireland, especially the acts of terrorism by unionist and nationalist groups, meant that the status quo was no longer an option. Since then British and Irish governments have tried, with varying degrees of success, to bring all sides together and end the 'troubles' for good.

....

✓ **What you should have learnt from reading this chapter**

- History is very important with respect to current events in Northern Ireland.

- The divide in religion is at the heart of the problems in Northern Ireland.

- The 1801 Act of Union between Ireland and Britain left Ireland with the status of a quasi-colony and soon resulted in resentment and a rise in nationalism.

- The potato famine in Ireland changed politics in Ireland for ever.

- Irish nationalism started as a political movement within the British political system but, with the failure to achieve Home Rule, it resulted in ever-increasing degrees of militancy and violence.

- Original Irish nationalism was a cause taken up by both Catholic and Protestant Irish. Over time, however, Unionism became the domain of Protestants and Nationalism that of Catholics.

- After the failure to achieve Home Rule in Northern Ireland, a bitter insurrection occurred in Ireland. The British government failed to suppress it and, as a result of the Government of Ireland Act, 1920 and the Treaty of Ireland, 1922, Northern and Southern Ireland were separated.

- The devolved parliament in Ulster, known as Stormont, set about creating a Protestant state supported by Unionism under the Orange Order.

- Despite clear evidence of the Protestant suppression of Catholics and their rights, the various governments at Westminster declined to interfere with devolved matters in Northern Ireland.

- The more liberal Ulster Unionist attempts at reform were resisted by the more militant unionists. The Catholics and some liberal Protestants began a civil-rights movement that was, in turn, suppressed by the government at Stormont.

- From 1968 onwards, Ulster spiralled into increasing violence and, over the coming decades, thousands would die through terrorism.

- Direct rule from London was imposed on Northern Ireland in 1972, and British and Irish governments looked for a peaceful settlement to the 'troubles' thereafter.

- In 1998 the British and Irish governments signed the 'Good Friday Agreement' which started a new, more peaceful phase in Northern Ireland's history.

Glossary of key terms

Catholic The word literally means 'universal'. The Roman Catholics see their faith as the faith of the Universal Church throughout the world. Since the fourth century AD, it has been centred on Rome in Italy. In terms of membership, it is the largest of the Christian Churches in Ireland and across the world.

Direct rule The governing of Ireland directly from Westminster and Whitehall, while the devolved government of Northern Ireland is suspended.

Ethnic cleansing The process of forcibly removing particular religious or ethnic groups from mixed areas leaving just one ethnic or religious group remaining.

Fenian movement Irish-American republican secret society formed in the United States in 1858 and named after the legendary Fianna, a band of armed warriors who protected the ancient High Kingdom of Ireland.

Protestant A Christian who does not follow the Roman Catholic Church and whose faith is based on that of Luther or Calvin. It is the general name given to the Christian Churches which broke away from the Roman Catholic Church after 1517. In the context of Northern Ireland, it is the Anglican Church which broke away from Rome under Henry VIII.

Single transferable vote (STV) A system of proportional voting based on the allocation of a voter's preferences to individual candidates. It is the voting system that most closely matches a political party's share of the votes to the number of seats it gains in the election. The system, however, is complex and election results are not immediately available.

Likely examination questions

Identify the key political events in Irish history that, in 1968, led to the start of the 'troubles'.

To what extent does the current political situation in Northern Ireland owe its origins to the events that occurred in the nineteenth and early twentieth centuries?

Examine the reasons why the peace process took decades to achieve any tangible results?

Helpful websites

http://www.bbc.co.uk/history/war/troubles/ The BBC history unit provides full details of the troubles.

http://www.schoolshistory.org.uk/Ireland/irelandlinks.htm A schools history website providing information on recent Northern Ireland history.

http://www.wesleyjohnston.com/users/ireland/past/history/19211925.html
A complete history of Northern Ireland.

http://www.bbc.co.uk/radio4/history/empire This Sceptred Isle, Empire
has a history of Ireland as a 'colony'.

 ## Suggestions for further reading

A. Aughey, and M. Duncan (eds), *Northern Ireland Politics*, Longman, 1996.

M. Cunningham, *British Government Policy in Northern Ireland*,
Manchester University Press, 2001.

E. Curtis, *A History of Ireland from Earliest Times to 1922*, Routledge, 1936.

R. Deacon, *Devolution in Britain Today*, Manchester University Press, 2006.

T. Hennessey, *The Northern Ireland Peace Process: Ending the Troubles?*,
Palgrave, 2001.

M. Muholland, *Northern Ireland: A Very Short Introduction*, Oxford
University Press, 2003.

P. Rose, *How the Troubles Came to Northern Ireland*, Palgrave, 2001.

J. Tonge, *The New Northern Irish Politics?*, Palgrave, 2005.

CHAPTER 10

Northern Ireland and Devolution: Structures and Process

Contents

Overview

Devolution within Northern Ireland has evolved in a different manner from devolution elsewhere within the United Kingdom. Hence, the structures and processes are unique and have had to be constructed in a more conciliatory fashion than the devolution settlements in Wales and Scotland. As mentioned in the previous chapter, central to the establishment of the actual structures of devolved government in Northern Ireland, are the peace process and the Good Friday Agreement. This chapter will focus initially, on some of the detail of the agreement before assessing the structures of government that arose from it.

Key issues to be covered in this chapter

- The Good Friday Agreement
- North and south devolution referendums
- Government structures in Northern Ireland
- Assembly and executive powers
- The workings of the d'Hondt electoral procedure
- Arms decommissioning
- Devolution in trouble: communications breakdown
- Restarting the assembly

The Good Friday Agreement

The **Good Friday Agreement** (GFA) was the name given to the political deal that aimed at creating a lasting political settlement, or **'lasting peace'** within Northern Ireland. It was signed on 19 April 1998. It marked the climax of a long political process involving statements, proclamations and face-to-face dialogue that had started as far back as the 1970s but which had accelerated rapidly in the early 1990s. These talks dealt with how Northern Ireland should be governed in the future to ensure that the aspirations of all Northern Ireland's communities could be accommodated in a democratic manner. A vital moment in the process came about with the IRA's announcement on 31 August 1994 that it would be ceasing to engage in further military operations. This enabled John Hume, leader of the nationalist SDLP, to intensify his talks with Gerry Adams of Sinn Fein. This episode highlights the delicate balance in Northern Ireland between democratic and non-democratic methods of attaining and maintaining power. It also displays how paramilitary forces have to be taken into the equation whenever there is any discussion about progressing the governance of Northern Ireland. Thus, with talk of 'peace not war', a new mood appeared to be reverberating around Northern Ireland.

Box 10.1 The Good Friday Agreement

The proposals settled on in the Good Friday Agreement included:

- Plans for a Northern Ireland Assembly with a power-sharing executive.
- New cross-border institutions involving the Irish Republic, and a body linking devolved assemblies across the United Kingdom with Westminster and Dublin.
- The Irish Republic was to drop its constitutional claim, in Articles 2 and 3 of the Republic's Constitution, to the six counties which form Northern Ireland.
- Proposals on the decommissioning of paramilitary weapons.
- Proposals on the future of policing in Northern Ireland.
- Proposals for the early release of paramilitary prisoners.

Source: www.news.bbc.co.uk

Four years on, and with many political highs and lows having been endured, the Good Friday Agreement passed into history.

When looked at in more detail, the Good Friday Agreement document stated that the Northern Ireland Assembly would be democratically elected and that no one party would be dominant; hence the commitment to '**power sharing**'. To these ends the GFA included safeguards for cross-community participation. This would show itself in the allocation of committee chairs, ministers and committee members in proportion to party strength.

When it came to dealing with matters that were not merely procedural, or strictly internal to Northern Ireland, the GFA laid out plans for the establishment of a North-South Ministerial Council whereby Belfast and Dublin could discuss matters of mutual interest. To avoid claims of any bias towards nationalists, it was laid out by the GFA that any decisions made by the North-South Council must be agreed by both sides. Similarly, a British-Irish Council was set up to encourage political, economic and cultural interaction between all peoples on the islands of Britain and Ireland. This was dubbed 'the Council of the Isles' by some commentators. It was envisaged that, when put into practice, this body would have representatives from the British and Irish governments, the devolved institutions in Northern Ireland, Scotland and Wales, and also representatives from the Isle of Man and the Channel Islands.

Furthermore a British-Irish Intergovernmental Conference was also to be established. This would comprise senior representatives from both governments, and it would meet to promote bilateral co-operation on every matter of mutual interest. Finally, a consultative Civic Forum would come into existence. This would comprise representatives of business, trade unions and other sectors in Northern Ireland. It was envisaged that this Civic Forum could act as a consultative mechanism on social, economic and cultural issues.

The Good Friday Agreement and respect for all

The **peace process** had sought to foster understanding between the different political, cultural and religious groups in Northern Ireland. Allied to this, more empathy had to be encouraged between people in Northern Ireland and those outside its borders. The GFA asked all the participants in the peace process and the GFA to affirm their commitment to achieving mutual respect through the upholding of the civil rights and the religious liberties of everyone in Northern Ireland and beyond. To embed this element of respect, the GFA brought forward measures to establish a new Northern Ireland Human Rights Commission and to legislate for the incorporation of the European Convention on Human Rights into Northern Ireland's law.

Following on from the section on human rights, the GFA turned its attention to the issue of the decommissioning of paramilitary weapons. It is this section that has proved to be the most contentious – as indeed it was from the outset – and difficult to apply. As will be mentioned later, the timescale for decommissioning, and the manner in which it is to be conducted, have proved to be very problematical. In similar terms, the GFA's position on policing in Northern Ireland, and the early release of paramilitary prisoners, assuming that the organisation to which they are attached were maintaining their ceasefires, has proved to be controversial.

The devolved assembly in Northern Ireland

The electorate of Northern Ireland endorsed the Good Friday Agreement in a referendum held on 22 May 1998. On the same day, voters in the Republic of Ireland accepted the changes to Articles 2 and 3 of the Republic's Constitution, which cast aside any territorial claims that the South may have had to the North. Table 10.1 shows the results.

The referendum's endorsement paved the way for the introduction of the Northern Ireland Act (1998). The act defined the future institutions of government in Northern Ireland, and laid down the principles for collaboration between the governments of Britain, the Republic of Ireland and the devolved assembly at Belfast. On 25 June 1998 elections to the new Northern Ireland Assembly were held with 108 Members being elected using the single transferable vote (STV) form of proportional representation (PR). Six representatives were returned from each of Northern Ireland's eighteen Westminster constituencies. Those elected are known as **Members of the Legislative Assembly** (MLAs). The figures for the 1998 Northern Ireland Assembly Election are shown in Table 10.2. The political parties that took part in the election will be analysed at length in the following chapter.

Table 10.1 The Good Friday Agreement referendums, 1998

	Yes	Percentage	No	Percentage	Turnout (percentage)
Northern Ireland (to support/ reject the GFA)	676,966	71.1	274,879	28.9	81.1
Republic of Ireland (to amend Articles 2 and 3)	1,442,583	94.4	85,748	5.6	56.3

Source: J. Tonge, *The New Northern Irish Politics?* (2005).

The assembly's powers

The assembly has full executive and legislative authority for all '**transferred matters**'. These transferred matters include areas such as education, health and agriculture. Policy fields, such as defence and taxation, remain '**excepted matters**', or 'matters of national importance' and are therefore not devolved to the Belfast institution.

Similarly to the Scottish Parliament, but unlike the Welsh Assembly, the Northern Ireland Assembly has the power to enact primary legislation for Northern Ireland. Proposals for legislation (or draft legislation) are referred to as 'bills' until they are firstly approved by the assembly, then accepted by the Secretary of State for Northern Ireland and, finally, given Royal Assent. When this process is complete the bills become acts.

Ministers, committees and individual members can propose a bill to the Speaker of the Northern Ireland Assembly for consideration by the assembly. If the Speaker is content that the proposals are within the assembly's competence the bill is then introduced and debated in the chamber. It is also scrutinised by the appropriate statutory committee. The committee then reports back to the assembly allowing members to consider the details of the bill and to propose

Table 10.2 Northern Ireland Assembly election, 1998

Party	First Preference Votes		
	Votes	Percentage	Seats
SDLP	177,963	22.0	24
UUP	172,917	21.3	28
DUP	145,917	18.1	20
SF	142,848	17.7	18
Alliance	52,636	6.5	6
UKUP	36,541	4.5	5
PUP	20,634	2.6	2
NIWC	13,019	1.6	2
Others	47,452	5.8	3*
Total	824,391		108
Turnout		69.95	

* Three independent Anti-Agreement Unionists.

Source: ESRC Election Briefing (2004).

amendments. It is then considered further by the assembly and a final vote is taken. If approved, the Speaker will ask the Secretary of State to seek Royal Assent to enable the bill to become an Act of the Northern Ireland Assembly.

Executive powers

Executive powers are concerned with the administration of public services – health, environment, etc. – and are discharged by the government departments (the Civil Service). The assembly delegates its executive powers to an Executive Committee made up of the First

Minister and Deputy First Minister. There is also one minister for each of the ten government departments. Members of the Executive Committee are appointed from the 108 MLAs, according to party strengths. Once in place, the Executive Committee forwards proposals for new legislation. It does this in the form of 'executive bills' that can be considered by the entire assembly. The Executive Committee also sets out a Programme for Government each year with a budget that has to be agreed by the assembly.

The assembly carries out its work in plenary (full) meetings of the assembly and by the work of assembly committees. Box 10.2 (overleaf) provides more information on these committees.

A first minister and a deputy first minister are elected to lead the Executive Committee of Ministers. They must stand for election jointly and, to be elected, they must have cross-community support by the 'parallel consent' formula. This means that a majority of both the members who have designated themselves nationalists and those who have designated themselves unionists, and a majority of the whole assembly, must vote in favour. This is a prime example of the quid pro quo character of the Good Friday Agreement and the consensual nature that has now become a mandatory part of Northern Ireland's political environment. However, One criticism of this 'parallel consent' formula, however, could be that, in its requirement that MLAs designate themselves along traditional nationalist/unionist lines, with the third category being a fairly nondescript 'other', they are merely perpetuating their own, and invariably their communities', embedded prejudices. This form of **'designation'** could therefore be seen as stifling as it does not allow politicians, and perhaps even communities, to alter and realign their ideological positions. If the GFA was all about creating a 'new politics' in Northern Ireland then, it could be argued, the 'designation' and 'parallel consent' clauses may not be its finest achievements.

The First Minister and Deputy First Minister head the Executive Committee of Ministers and, acting together, they determine the total number of ministers in the executive. Having done this, the parties elected to the assembly choose ministerial portfolios and select ministers in proportion to their party strength. Each party has a designated nominating officer and the 'd'Hondt procedure' is used for the appointment of ministers.

Box 10.2 Northern Ireland Assembly: meeting and committee structure

- **Plenary meetings** of the assembly are usually held twice a week (on Mondays and Tuesdays) in the assembly chamber.
- **Statutory committees** A statutory committees shadows each of the ten Northern Ireland government departments. The committees have the power to examine and to recommend changes to departmental policies. They can also initiate legislation. Furthermore, statutory committees may carry out independent investigations into any current issue that ministers may be considering.
- **Standing committees** Six standing committees were established by the assembly to assist it in its work These cover issues such as finance, procedures, and assembly business.
- **Ad hoc committees** These are set up, as and when they are needed, to undertake a specific task or piece of work.
- **Office holders** Committee chairs, and those who wish to act as members of the various committees, are appointed using a selection system that ensures each party in the assembly is represented according to the votes it received in the election. The eleven members of each statutory committee, including the Chair and Deputy Chair, are also appointed in a way that reflects party representation in the assembly, and the Chair and Deputy Chair do not normally belong to the same political party as the relevant departmental minister.

Source: www.niassembly.gov.uk

The d'Hondt route to consensus politics

With a premium being put on inclusive, consensus politics in the 'new' Northern Ireland, the GFA decided to adopt the '**d'Hondt procedure**', or 'highest average method'. Named after a nineteenth-century Belgian lawyer, the idea is that a party's total vote is divided by a certain figure which increases as it wins more seats. As the diviser becomes bigger, then the party's total in succeeding rounds gets smaller, allowing parties with lower initial totals to win seats. By initiating d'Hondt, no single party should be able to dominate or control the proceedings of the assembly. In reality the method of appointing ministers by this allocation system has come in for some criticism from observers of the process. It is not so much that the idea of achieving a fair balance is wrong in itself, it receives criticism because certain ministers, feeling secure in their new posts, have gone on to use their departments as 'power bases' from which they have pursued their individual agendas, or those of their party, rather than associating their department with the agreed line of the executive or the assembly. This goes against the notion of the co-operative, collaborative, 'joined-up' government that the Good Friday Agreement envisaged.

The early days of the Northern Ireland Assembly were marred by a series of political rows and delays. Despite the failure to form an executive by July 1999, the assembly met on the fifteenth of that month to activate the d'Hondt procedure. Alas, only Sinn Fein and the SDLP made nominations. Since ministers could hold office only if their nominations included three designated Unionists and three designated Nationalists the conditions for the appointment had not been met and the assembly was adjourned. This is an example of where the 'designation' principle succeeded in halting, rather than progressing, the operation of the assembly.

The above case is just one example of the extremely long teething time that the assembly underwent. United States Senator George Mitchell was called in to oversee a review of the political process, and things appeared to get moving when the assembly met on 29 November 1999, and ministers and chairs were agreed upon. The following day, 30 November, the Secretary of State issued the Northern Ireland Act 1998 (Commencement Order No. 5), resulting in the devolution of powers to the Northern Ireland Assembly from 2 December 1999. Upon the final granting of devolution, Lord Alderdice of the Alliance Party was confirmed as Speaker and he continued in that capacity until his retirement on 29 February 2004.

Up and running! The assembly after devolution

With the assembly now sitting, and with its powers devolved from Westminster, it may have appeared that this would be the assembly's 'honeymoon period'. Many issues still remained unresolved, however, not least of which was the issue of weapons decommissioning. On 11 February 2000, the then Secretary of State, Peter Mandelson MP, signed an order to suspend the assembly and restore 'direct rule'. Mandelson was forced into taking this action because David Trimble, leader of the Ulster Unionist Party (UUP) and First Minister, threatened to resign and throw the devolution process into further disarray. It took until May 2000 for the deadlock to be broken. On 6 May the Provisional IRA released a statement saying that it was ready to begin a process that would 'completely and verifiably' put its arms beyond use. In fact it would be another fifteen months, in August 2001, before the International Commission on Decommissioning, headed by General John de Chastelain, could state that the IRA had forwarded a plan to put its weapons 'beyond use'. Nevertheless, after the statement of 6 May, David Trimble did consult his party which then agreed that Trimble and the UUP should re-enter the power-sharing assembly. This was an early indicator of the stop-start nature of devolved politics in Northern Ireland.

Decommissioning and David Trimble

The continuing argument about decommissioning led, eventually, to the resignation of David Trimble as First Minister on 1 July 2001, to be followed, on 18 October, by other UUP ministers. During this phase many decisions were taken directly by the Secretary of State and Downing Street as this was a period of indecision and confusion. After a lot of behind-the-scenes manoeuvring, David Trimble was eventually re-elected as First Minister on 5 November 2001, along with the SDLP's Mark Durkan as Deputy Minister to replace Seamus Mallon who had retired. Trimble's return as First Minister came about after pro-Agreement parties had struck a deal to re-elect him by redesignating three Alliance Party MLAs as unionists.

Open again for business!

In the eleven months from November 2001 to October 2002, the Northern Ireland Assembly did make progress on a number of issues. The assembly, the executive and the committees met regularly and consensus was reached on most matters. Business transacted in this period included the following:

- The Executive produced a draft Programme for Government (subtitled 'Reinvestment and Reform'), and a draft budget for 2003–4 was agreed.
- The various committees published nearly fifty reports on such diverse subjects as the outbreak of foot-and-mouth disease in Northern Ireland, child protection, tourism, fur farming, homelessness, and water management.
- The assembly debated and passed seventeen acts in 2001 and fourteen in 2002. MLAs also began the practice of presenting public petitions on constituency-related issues.
- There were many important debates on topics such as the NHS, the future of education in Northern Ireland, the work of the Children's Commissioner, and telecommunications in Ulster.
- MLAs raised matters of importance in their own constituencies by means of adjournment debates.

Communication breakdown: devolution in trouble

On 4 October 2002 Sinn Fein's offices at **Stormont** were raided as part of a major police investigation into alleged intelligence-gathering by republicans. Ten days later, amid an environment of accusations and political tension, Secretary of State, John Reid MP, announced that devolution was to be suspended from midnight and that the return of 'direct rule' would follow.

Although elections to the Northern Ireland Assembly were held in November 2003 (see Table 10.3) with the DUP and Sinn Fein topping the unionist and nationalist community votes respectively, devolved government, in a formal sense, remained 'on hold'.

In 2004, a series of intergovernmental and cross-party talks was held in an attempt to break the deadlock and to set in motion, once again, the devolution process in Northern Ireland. Talks in Belfast were followed by three days of intensive negotiations at Leeds Castle in Kent with both the British Prime Minister, Tony Blair, and the Irish Taoiseach, Bertie Ahern, playing prominent roles. Though no agreement came out of the Leeds Castle talks, a

Table 10.3 Northern Ireland Assembly election, 2003

Party	First Preference Votes		
	Votes	Percentage	Seats
DUP	177,944	25.7	30 (33)*
SF	162,758	23.5	24
UUP	156,931	22.7	27 (24)*
SDLP	117,547	16.98	18
Alliance	25,372	3.68	6
PUP	8,032	1.16	1
Ind.	6,158	0.88	1†
NIWC	5,785	0.83	0
UKUP	5,700	0.82	1
Others	25,801	3.70	0
Total	692,028		108
Turnout		63.1	

* Jeffrey Donaldson, Arlene Foster and Norah Beare left the UUP to join the DUP on 5 January 2004.
† Dr Kieran Deeny (West Tyrone). Dr Deeny ran on a single issue: the retention of acute hospital services in Omagh, Co. Tyrone. He topped the poll in the constituency, attracting first preference votes from both union- ist and nationalist electors.

Source: *ESRC Election Briefing* (2004).

more optimistic mood emerged among politicians who felt that the assembly could soon resume its business. The issue of weapons decommissioning still loomed large, however, and unionist demands for photographic evidence of IRA decommissioning created another political row.

The stalemate continues – 2005

Despite a high-profile intervention from United States President, George Bush, at the end of 2004, to try to persuade all sides in the dispute to settle their differences and move on, little real progress was made towards resuming devolution at Stormont. In May 2005 two important events occurred in the British general election, UUP Leader David Trimble lost his Westminster seat of Upper Bann, and Peter Hain replaced Paul Murphy as Secretary of State. In July 2005, the IRA declared that its armed campaign was over and talked about replacing it with democratic political activities. The response from Downing Street was to announce a two-year plan to scale down the British Army's presence in Northern Ireland and to reduce the number of troops based in Ulster from 10,500 to 5,000. Unionists, unsurprisingly, claimed that the British government was playing into the hands of the nationalists.

Time for action – 2006

By 2006 there was an air of desperation about government circles in London and Dublin. In April 2006, after another breakdown in talks between the interested parties, Tony Blair and Bertie Ahern attempted to set out a timetable for restoring devolution for Northern Ireland. In the timetable, the assembly would be recalled on 15 May with the express purpose of electing first and deputy first ministers and agreeing an executive within six weeks. MLAs would then be given until 24 November to set up a new power-sharing executive. If this did not materialise, then MLAs' salaries – £41,321 per MLA per annum when the assembly is sitting but £31,817 during suspension – would be stopped and the British and Irish governments would then work on partnership arrangements to implement the Good Friday Agreement. Summarising the plan, therefore, the restoration of devolution would occur only if three conditions are met:

- a first and deputy first minister are elected with cross-party consent;
- an executive is elected with similar cross-party support;
- all persons elected have affirmed the terms of the assembly's pledge of office.

To show their commitment to this plan, Blair and Ahern issued a joint statement at Navan Fort, Armagh. Secretary of State, Peter Hain, then announced on 18 April that emergency legislation would go before the houses of Parliament. The bill received Royal Assent on 8 May. On 15 May, in an assembly meeting that lasted just fourteen minutes, Sinn Fein President, Gerry Adams, talking in Gaelic, nom-inated Ian Paisley as First Minister and Sinn Fein's Martin McGuinness as Deputy First Minister. Unsurprisingly, Paisley dismissed this suggestion and the meeting came to an end. Secretary of State Peter Hain's response to these events was to talk of initiating a 'virtual assembly' in order to overcome the impasse. Here, the assembly could meet and debate but it would not pass legislation. Hain's hope was that a level of trust would build up among the MLAs and, out of this, would come a compromise that would see the 'real' assembly coming back into play.

Although the next election for the assembly is due in May 2007, provisions within the Northern Ireland Act 2000 allow for a year's postponement to permit the restarted assembly to 'bed itself in' without the disruption of an election period. This, naturally, presumes that all the contesting parties currently represented in the assembly will agree to move forward and reignite the devolution process. Past experiences, however, may weigh against such optimism.

∙∙

✓ What you should have learnt from reading this chapter

- The Good Friday Agreement was not universally welcomed across Northern Ireland.

- While the peace process is considered to be an event of the 1990s, in reality clandestine talks to end the troubles had been going on since the 1970s.

- The fact that referendums on differing, but very much related, issues had to be held in Ulster and the Republic on the same day in 1998 demonstrates the historically political complexities of the situation in Northern Ireland.

- Cross-party co-operation in Northern Ireland is exceptionally difficult to achieve.

Glossary of key terms

Designation Part of the assembly process whereby MLAs categorise themselves in ideological terms. They do so, predominantly, along nationalist and unionist lines.

D'Hondt procedure A method for electing ministers that is meant to ensure a fair allocation of seats based on a party's actual strength in terms of the number of votes it secures.

Excepted matters Policy areas that are not devolved to the Northern Ireland Assembly but remain the preserve of the Westminster government.

Good Friday Agreement The concord that was signed on Good Friday 1998. It was designed to ensure a peaceful future for Northern Ireland through inclusive democratic government.

Lasting peace The idea that any ceasefires or intentions to disarm by paramilitary forces should pave the way towards the demilitarisation of Northern Ireland in order that the province may live peacefully for the foreseeable future.

Member of the Legislative Assembly (MLA) MLAs are the elected representatives who sit in the Northern Ireland Assembly at Stormont.

Peace process The term 'peace process' generally refers to the period in the 1990s which saw political dialogue at party, community and governmental level that was aimed at achieving a 'lasting peace' in Northern Ireland.

Power sharing A built-in mechanism that operates in an institution to make sure that no one group or party dominates proceedings.

Stormont The Stormont building in Belfast is the site of the Northern Ireland Assembly.

Transferred matters Policy areas, such as education and health, that have been devolved from Westminster to Stormont.

Likely examination questions

Discuss why the peace process is 'ongoing' rather than settled.

How likely is it that Northern Ireland will become demilitarised in the near future?

Consider why devolution has proved to be such a stop-start process in Northern Ireland.

Helpful websites

www.niassembly.gov.uk the Northern Ireland Assembly.

www.belfasttelegraph.co.uk for more information about politics in Northern Ireland.

Suggestions for further reading

A. Little, *Democracy and Northern Ireland: Beyond the Liberal Paradigm*, Palgrave, 2004.

J. Neuheiser and S. Wolff (eds), *Peace at Last?*, Berghahn Books, 2002.

CHAPTER 11

Political Parties within Northern Ireland

Contents

Overview

The political parties operating within Northern Ireland differ in several respects from those in existence in other parts of the United Kingdom. The crucial element missing within mainland Britain is the religious one. However, As is the case with Scotland and Wales, however, Northern Irish politics also differs in other ways. This chapter will analyse the history, key players and ideologies of the major political parties in Northern Ireland.

Key issues to be covered in this chapter

- The genealogy of the political parties in Northern Ireland
- Unionist, nationalist and non-aligned parties
- Party ideology and identities
- Key players: Gerry Adams and the Reverend Ian Paisley
- Coalition, co-operation and the centre ground

The genealogy of political parties in Northern Ireland

Most political parties in Northern Ireland have been formed from within the religious communities in Ulster – hence their link to **sectarianism** – and their formation has often been in response to some political or historical event. For instance, the formations of **Sinn Fein** and the **Ulster Unionist Party** at the beginning of twentieth century were indicative of the rising political and religious tensions that were evident at that time. Likewise, the arrival of the **SDLP**, the **DUP**, and the **Alliance Party** at the start of the 1970s highlights that period's turbulent political environment. With this as a backdrop, this chapter will now look in more detail at some of the specific parties operating in Ulster.

Unionist political parties

Unionist political parties are those that support maintaining the Union between Ulster and mainland Britain. These parties are mostly, though not always, supported by members of the Protestant community. Thus, they tend to reflect all the different shades of Protestant political and religious thinking.

Box 11.1 Formation and ideologies of political parties in Northern Ireland

- 1905: Ulster Unionist Party (unionist/traditional conservative)
- 1905: Sinn Fein (republican/socialist)
- 1970: SDLP (nationalist/social democrat)
- 1970: Alliance Party (non-sectarian/liberal)
- 1971: Democratic Unionist Party (unionist/staunchly patriotic)
- 1979: Progressive Unionist Party (loyalist/proletarian)
- 1996: UK Unionist Party (moderate loyalist/eurosceptic)
- 1996: Northern Ireland Women's Coalition (non-sectarian/radical)

Source: www.cain.ulst.ac.uk

Democratic Unionist Party (DUP)

The Democratic Unionist Party (DUP) was formed in 1971. Its leader is, and has been since its formation, the Reverend Ian Paisley MP, MLA, and former MEP. Paisley is also a Presbyterian minister and his political and religious oratories are often interwoven. Indeed, Paisley's unique position in Northern Ireland politics and society is assured through his founding of the Free Presbyterian Church, in 1951, and the Democratic Unionist Party.

The fight for God and Ulster

The DUP presents itself as the only alternative to Sinn Fein, and it contends that Sinn Fein will become the largest party in Northern Ireland if the unionist vote is evenly split. Therefore, contend Paisley and the DUP, the only way to preserve unionist and Protestant culture in Ulster is to vote DUP in order, as Paisley would see it, to marginalise the 'soft' unionist stance of the Ulster Unionist Party (UUP) and to counteract the republican agenda of those in the nationalist camp. This has been the party's message for years, and the DUP opposed the Good Friday Agreement because it said that the deal, if implemented in full, would mean the end of the union between Britain and Northern Ireland. Although it has engaged in dialogue since, the DUP refused to take part in negotiations which, it maintained, would lead to rule from Dublin. For the DUP, therefore, the fight throughout the peace process has been about maintaining political and religious traditions and values. To paraphrase, it is about 'God and Ulster'.

Interestingly, the European dimension is one that the DUP plays up as it sees an additional level of bureaucracy and interference emanating from Brussels. It is little surprise, therefore, that the DUP opposes the introduction of the Euro to Britain and campaigns against 'the further encroachment of Europe in our national affairs'. Tying this in with the Britian-wide programme for devolution, the DUP has been very critical of the Labour Party under Tony Blair and the 'constitutional vandalism' that it perceives to haven taken place since 1997.

The DUP currently has nine MPs at Westminster and thirty-three MLAs (this figure includes three MLAs who were elected as Ulster Unionists but who subsequently defected to the DUP). Thus, it is currently the leading party in Northern Ireland, both in terms of unionism and in terms of overall number of votes cast and seats won.

Box 11.2 Key figures: Reverend Ian Paisley

- Born 1926
- Ordained as a minister in 1946
- Founded the Free Presbyterian Church in 1951
- Demanded the removal of an Irish tricolour in Belfast in 1964
- Regularly criticises the practices of the Pope and the Roman Catholic Church
- 1971: Established the intransigently loyal Democratic Unionist Party
- 1974: Elected to Westminster
- 1979: Became a Member of the European Parliament
- Vehemently opposed any alliances between North and South that were being suggested in the 1980s.
- Opposed the Good Friday Agreement but has been forced slightly to moderate his position about 'power-sharing' with nationalists
- Elected as an MLA in 1998; re-elected in 2003
- May 2006: Turned down the chance to become First Minister of Northern Ireland after being nominated for the post by Gerry Adams

Ulster Unionist Party (UUP)

Formed across the whole of Ireland, in 1905, in order to counter the threat posed by the Home Rule movement, the UUP has been, until recently, the dominant unionist grouping in Irish politics. It ruled Northern Ireland, in the old Stormont Parliament, from 1921 to 1972. Although it saw itself as driving a pro-monarchist and pro-unionist agenda during that period, its policies were actually seen by many commentators as heavily favouring the Protestant community over the Catholic one. This apparent anti-Catholic bias helped to instigate the civil rights campaigns of the 1960s.

The UUP has long been seen as the most traditionalist and establishment-based party in Northern Ireland. This is due in part to the fact that many of its leaders have come from the armed forces or from the professions. From Colonel Edward Saunderson in 1905 through Sir Basil Brooke after World War II to Captain Terence O'Neill in the 1960s, a patrician-style of leadership has been in evidence.

The UUP and moderation
Despite its conservative stance on most issues, the UUP has proved to be the most conciliatory party within the unionist grouping. Moves by other political organisations have forced the UUP to realise that arguing for the status quo in Northern Ireland is no longer an option. Therefore, the UUP's willingness to negotiate with various bodies, such as the government of the Irish Republic, the SDLP, and even Sinn Fein, can be seen as being both pragmatic and an acknowledgment that the party's ideological positioning was becoming more moderate.

At the time of the peace process, the leader of the UUP was David Trimble. After ten years at the helm, Trimble stepped down from office in May 2005 following the UUP's disappointing showing at the 2005 General Election when it returned only one MP. Also, in 2005, after decades of having a close working relationship with the Orange Order, the order distanced itself from the UUP. Commentators read this as a sign that the Orange Order had lost patience with the UUP, and that many Orangemen disliked the UUP's moderate stance towards 'power-sharing' with republican politicians. At the moment, the UUP has twenty-four MLAs, and the party is currently led by Sir Reg Empey, MLA for Belfast East.

Progressive Unionist Party (PUP)
The **Progressive Unionist Party** (PUP) is one of the smaller unionist parties functioning in Northern Ireland. The PUP was formed in 1979 out of the Independent Unionist Group whose base was in the Shankill Road area of Belfast. The PUP differs from the larger unionist parties in that it has links to the paramilitary organisation, the **Ulster Volunteer Force** (UVF).

Owing to the PUP's close identification with the Protestant working classes, it is sometimes referred to as the 'left-wing' party of unionism, unionism tending to be associated with more traditionalist and conservative ideologies. Despite its controversial ties to a paramilitary organisation, in recent years PUP has argued for what it calls a 'sharing of responsibility' between unionists and nationalists. Hence, the PUP maintains that Northern Ireland cannot be governed without some posts on the executive being reserved for nationalists.

The PUP was led, until his death in January 2007, by David Ervine who proved to be one of the strongest supporters of the Good Friday

Agreement. He represented the constituency of Belfast East. The PUP also has two local councillors. With the reconvening of the Northern Ireland Assembly in May 2006, albeit in 'virtual' form, Ervine pledged to join the UUP assembly group while remaining a PUP MLA. This 'marriage of convenience' would entitle the Ulster Unionists, under the d'Hondt formula, to an additional place on the Northern Ireland Executive.

United Kingdom Unionist Party (UKUP)

The **United Kingdom Unionist Party** is an anti-devolution unionist party that contends that Northern Ireland should become 'more British'. To this extent UKUP is integrationist, as it believes that Northern Ireland should be governed from London with no regional or devolved government in Belfast. Given this idea, it is not surprising that the party is very much against the Good Friday Agreement and it particularly opposes any political and constitutional links with the Republic of Ireland.

UKUP was set up – nominally in 1995 but then in reconstituted form in 1996 – to contest the 1996 elections for the Northern Ireland Forum. These were elections to see who would be represented in all-party talks as part of the peace process. The instigator of this new party was former UUP politician Robert McCartney, QC. McCartney won the seat of North Down in a parliamentary by-election in 1995 when he stood as a 'UK Unionist'. Following his success, McCartney decided to launch the UK Unionist Party and was quickly, and somewhat surprisingly, supported by the writer and politician Conor Cruise O'Brien, a former minister in the Irish Republic. This helped to reinforce UKUP's claim that it was a non-sectarian unionist party.

UKUP's policies

Apart from its unionist position, UKUP has also adopted a staunchly anti-European line. It has allied itself with the UK Independence Party which favours Britain's withdrawal from the European Union. UKUP maintains that one of its core pledges to voters is that it would keep the pound sterling and reject the Euro. The party has also campaigned against the downgrading of traditional aspects and symbols of life in Northern Ireland. One such move that upset UKUP was the reorganising of policing in Northern Ireland. The party disliked the idea that the established Royal Ulster Constabulary (RUC) was to be renamed and re-branded as the Police Service of Northern Ireland (PSNI).

In electoral terms, five UKUP candidates became MLAs in the Northern Ireland Assembly Election in 1998. After some turbulent internal debates regarding UKUP's position on Sinn Fein's participation in assembly matters, Robert McCartney incensed his colleagues with some of his proposals. So much so, indeed, that all four of them left to form the Northern Ireland Unionist Party. As for McCartney, he lost his Westminster seat at the 2001 General Election but managed narrowly to retain his assembly seat in 2003. Meanwhile, all four of McCartney's former colleagues, now in the Northern Ireland Unionist Party, lost their seats.

Nationalist political parties

Nationalist political parties take the opposite line to unionist parties when it comes to the preservation of the union between Ulster and Britain. Nationalist political parties wish to see a united Ireland; they disagree, however, on the pace and method of achieving this goal.

The Social Democratic and Labour Party (SDLP)

The Social Democratic and Labour Party (SDLP) was formed in 1970 by activists operating within the Labour movement in Northern Ireland and in left-of-centre politics generally. Many of its first members were also experienced in the campaign for civil rights for Roman Catholics. From its formation in 1970 up to the 2001 General Election, the SDLP was the dominant voice of nationalist politics in Northern Ireland. At present, however, it is the smaller of the two main nationalist parties, having lost ground to Sinn Fein in recent years.

In terms of its ideology, the SDLP is a social democratic party that believes in the parliamentary and constitutional road to a united Ireland; hence, the party's persistent opposition to the paramilitary campaign of the Provisional IRA. As its name suggests, social democracy is crucial to the party's objectives but, from time to time, it is also keen to stress its nationalist credentials. For example, from the early 1970s onwards, the SDLP laid emphasis on what it called the 'Irish dimension'. Controversially, so far as unionists were concerned, this called for the Republic of Ireland to have not only a say in Northern Irish politics but a defined constitutional role. The perpetual nationalist/socialist debate has claimed its victims throughout the SDLP's history. Most notably, in 1979, Gerry Fitt, the SDLP's first leader and formerly leader of the explicitly socialist Republican Labour Party, resigned claiming that the party had become more nationalist than socialist for his liking. On a Europe-wide level, the SDLP is associated with the Party of European Socialists while, in global terms, it aligns itself with the Socialist International. Nearer home, the SDLP has traditionally had close links with the British Labour Party.

John Hume and inclusive politics

The leading figure in SDLP politics has been John Hume. A long-time advocate of a joint-authority approach to Northern Ireland's governance, where both the Republic of Ireland and Britain would exercise political power, throughout the 1980s and 1990s, Hume was instrumental in pushing the moderate nationalist case. Similarly, during this period, he ensured that the SDLP supported the Anglo-Irish Agreement, and he managed to persuade Sinn Fein to become more closely involved in constitutional politics. For his efforts, and with co-recipient David Trimble, Hume was eventually awarded the Nobel Peace Prize, for his substantial contribution to the peace process and to the signing of the Good Friday Agreement.

Hume stepped down from office in 2001, and the current SDLP leader is Mark Durkan, MLA for the Foyle constituency (see Box 11.3). Lately Durkan and the SDLP have argued that if, or when, a United Ireland comes about, the rights and protection of unionists must be guaranteed. The party supports the idea of a referendum to determine whether the people desire the establishment of a unified Irish state. The date for this referendum would be set when the institutions brought about by the Good Friday Agreement are seen to be operating in a stable and uninterrupted manner.

Box 11.3 Key figures: Mark Durkan

- Born in Derry in 1960
- Joined the SDLP in 1981
- Became a vital figure in policy planning in the 1980s
- Elected Chair of the SDLP in 1990
- Key member of the SDLP negotiation team in the run-up to the Good Friday Agreement
- Elected to the Northern Ireland Assembly in 1998
- Became Minister for Finance and Personnel in the Northern Ireland Executive
- 2001: Replaced Seamus Mallon as Deputy First Minister
- 2001: Elected leader of the SDLP
- 2003: Re-elected to the NI Assembly
- 2005: Won impressive majority in the Foyle seat at the Westminster election

Despite losing some electoral ground to Sinn Fein, the SDLP is still a major player within the politics of Northern Ireland. Since devolution, and more specifically since Durkan took over the leadership reins, the SDLP has been talking more and more about '**outreach**' into the unionist communities to ensure that Protestants and unionists are reassured about their future roles within the politics of Ireland. This conciliatory rhetoric may well be genuine – and Mark Durkan himself has addressed the Protestant and unionist community on this issue – but it is nevertheless viewed with a great deal of suspicion by many unionist politicians. The SDLP currently has three MPs in the House of Commons and eighteen MLAs in the Northern Ireland Assembly. There is also the possibility that, in the near future, the party will seek a greater role for itself in the politics of the Republic and it has advocated its participation in debates in the Irish parliament, the Dáil Éireann.

Sinn Fein (SF)

Originally formed in 1905, Sinn Fein Gaelic for 'Ourselves Alone' was founded with the aim of separating Ireland from Britain in order to establish an Irish Republic. In the 1918 Westminster elections, in the aftermath of the 1916 Easter Rising, Sinn Fein won seventy-three out of the 105 Irish seats. While the setting-up of the Irish Republic in 1921 pleased some within the party, a sizeable minority, upset that Ulster had been allowed to stay under British sovereignty, continued to campaign for a united Ireland. The party, however, lost its early momentum and it became a minor force in Irish politics until the start of 'the troubles' in the 1960s.

There were splits within Sinn Fein in 1970 that saw the emergence of traditional and provisional branches. Arguing for immediate withdrawal of the British presence from Northern Ireland, Provisional Sinn Fein was more relevant at the time than the Official Sinn Fein movement and, in co-ordination with the Marxist-inspired Provisional IRA that had been established in 1969 to defend Catholic areas, a new radical activist style of politics was brought into play. From this time, on, it became the common understanding of politicians and journalist alike that Sinn Fein was acting as the political wing of the Provisional IRA. Hence the constant unionist references to 'Sinn Fein/IRA'.

Hunger strikes and 'dual strategy'

Sinn Fein grew as an organisation during the 1970s and 1980s and was at the forefront of Northern Ireland politics during some of its darkest days. During the IRA hunger strikes of the early 1980s, many in the nationalist community appreciated the way that Sinn Fein represented the aims of the hunger strikers, though this did not necessarily translate into votes for Sinn Fein. Gerry Adams (see Box 11.4), President of Sinn Fein since 1983, also came to prominence during these controversial times. It was Adams, spurred on by the election victory of one hunger striker, Bobby Sands, as MP for Fermanagh-South Tyrone, who saw that Sinn Fein could become a major political player. Adams's own election victory in West Belfast in 1983 marked a breakthrough for the party and gave credence, as far as Sinn Fein was concerned, to the dual **'Armalite and ballot box'** strategy. Looking back, there is no doubt that Adams, and Sinn Fein's, growing popularity alarmed the London and Dublin governments, and the Anglo-Irish Agreement of 1985, and the subsequent peace process, could be portrayed as attempts to curb republicanism. Once it became absorbed in all party talks and in the peace process, Sinn Fein, led by Adams and supported by chief negotiator, Martin

Box 11.4 Key figures: Gerry Adams

- Born 1948 in West Belfast
- Civil rights activist in the 1960s
- Interned without trial in 1972
- On his release in July 1972, Adams was involved in secret talks between the IRA and the British government that led to a brief ceasefire
- Imprisoned from 1973 to 1976
- Played leading political role during the hunger strikes of 1981
- Elected MP for West Belfast in 1983 with a majority of over 5,000
- In 1987 Adams was instrumental in the publication of the Sinn Fein document, *Scenario for Peace*
- Lost West Belfast to the SDLP in 1992
- Regained West Belfast in 1997
- Elected to the Northern Ireland Assembly in 1998; re-elected in 2003
- May 2006: courts controversy by proposing Ian Paisley as First Minister for the Northern Ireland Assembly

McGuinness, succeeded in dropping the 'Armalite' component of the dual strategy in favour of the 'ballot box'. The vital component in this new policy, however, was the Provisional IRA's initial ceasefire, and its declaration of an end to hostilities.

As the major nationalist grouping in Northern Ireland, at the present time, Sinn Fein has five MPs at Westminster, although they do not take their seats in the House of Commons because they refuse to swear an oath of allegiance to the Queen as Britain's Head of the State. Furthermore, the party has twenty-four MLAs and five Teachtai Dala (TDs), members of the Dáil Éireann. At the European Parliament they have two MEPs representing the constituencies of Dublin and the Six Counties.

Non-aligned, or non-sectarian, political parties

These parties attempt to offer political rather than politico-religious solutions to the problems facing the people of Northern Ireland today. They are sometimes referred to as 'bi-confessional' which means that they reflect the concerns of both of the major communities – Protestant and Catholic – in Northern Ireland.

The Alliance Party of Northern Ireland (Alliance)

Founded in 1970, the Alliance Party of Northern Ireland is a cross-community- and non-sectarian-based political party. Its remit, it claims, is to work on behalf of all sections of the community in Northern Ireland. To this extent, the party extols the ideals of equality of citizenship, diversity and social justice. The Alliance also talks about creating a harmonious and prosperous society in Northern Ireland through the championing and implementation of the fundamental principles of the Good Friday Agreement. Allied to Liberal International, the Alliance is strongly committed to the worldwide promotion of a human rights agenda.

The Alliance has a tradition of encouraging multi-party agreements and compromises. The party, for example, was an enthusiastic supporter of the Sunningdale Agreement, which collapsed under pressure in 1974. This was the forerunner of the Good Friday Agreement, which sought a three-stranded approach to Northern Ireland's governance that involved an executive and assembly in Ulster, cross-border co-operation and London-Dublin arrangements. Despite the collapse of Sunningdale, the Alliance's policy of creating 'one community' in Northern Ireland has seen it advocate 'power-sharing' options whenever they have arisen. Indeed, the Alliance has claimed that, despite the party's overall support for the Good Friday Agreement, parts of it should be renegotiated or rewritten to break down the unionist/nationalist bloc designations.

David Ford is the present leader of the Alliance. Ford, a keen advocate of **internationalism**, is the MLA for Antrim South. In December 2005 it was announced that the Alliance's Eileen Bell would stand down as Deputy Leader. Since then, Bell has been nominated for the position of Presiding Officer (Speaker) of the Northern Ireland Assembly which reconvened in virtual form on 15 May.

Northern Ireland Women's Coalition (NIWC)

Founded in 1996, the **Northern Ireland Women's Coalition** (NIWC) has brought a fresh approach to the politics of Ulster. Despite its title, NIWC is not just a female-only organisation and it does not adopt an overtly feminist line. The party, which tends to attract support from a middle-class base, seeks to promote cross-community politics and to reconcile differences between the different cultural and religious factions in Northern Ireland. NIWC talks of fostering a pluralist political environment where all groups, sexes, and ages can play their part; indeed, one of the reasons for establishing NIWC was to confront the perception many people had of Northern Ireland as being a male-dominated society.

NIWC has been supportive of the Good Friday Agreement and it sees it, somewhat optimistically, as a mechanism through which sectarianism can be challenged. Buoyed up by its participation in the peace process and the GFA, the Women's Coalition contested eight seats at the 1998 assembly election and won two of them. By 2003, however, its vote fell substantially, and it failed to gain representation. Having made an impact early on, the party must now reinvigorate itself and emphasise its strengths as a centrist, non-sectarian organisation if it is to regain the ground it lost in 2003.

What you should have learnt from reading this chapter

- Political parties in Northern Ireland have traditionally been centred on religious communities and politico-religious themes.

- Non-sectarian political parties are now established within Northern Ireland, though their message can remain marginalised at times.

- In recent years the political spectrum in Northern Ireland has swung firstly in favour of moderation and then against it.

- Despite the introduction of the Northern Ireland Women's Coalition, politics in Northern Ireland remains a male-dominated arena.

- Key political figures like Gerry Adams and the Reverend Ian Paisley have a huge influence on the political environment of Ulster.

Glossary of key terms

Alliance Party of Northern Ireland The main non-sectarian political party in Northern Ireland. The party is liberal in its political outlook.
'Armalite and ballot box' Sinn Fein's dual strategy of the 1980s and early 1990s that saw the party advocating the armed struggle combined with engagement with the democratic political process.

Democratic Unionist Party (DUP) The unionist political party, led by the Reverend Ian Paisley, that attracts most of its support from the grassroots Protestant community.

Internationalism The stance that other nations and cultures need to be fully respected and that people and governments of all colours and creeds should co-operate with each other.

Northern Ireland Women's Coalition Non-sectarian political party set up at the time of the peace process to offer the voice of women in a male-dominated political environment.

Outreach Moves by one community or political party to engage in dialogue or activities with another community or political party. Outreach is seen by many observers of Northern Ireland politics as being idealistic and ambitious.

Progressive Unionist Party (PUP) Minority unionist party whose support stems from people who would regard themselves as loyalists.

Sectarianism Community and political affiliation that manifests itself along strictly religious grounds. At the height of 'the troubles' murders were often referred to as 'sectarian killings'.

Sinn Fein (SF) Republican political organisation, and the largest nationalist grouping in the North, which advocates a united Ireland.

Social Democratic and Labour Party (SDLP) The mainstream Catholic and nationalist political party. Formerly the largest nationalist party.

United Kingdom Unionist Party (UKUP) Small Euro-sceptic unionist party that allies itself to the UK Independence Party.

Ulster Unionist Party (UUP) Long-time leading political force within unionist politics. Generally seen as a more middle-class and professionally based party than the DUP.

Ulster Volunteer Force (UVF) Loyalist paramilitary group, formed in 1966, which has links with the Progressive Unionist Party.

[?] Likely examination questions

Explain why the establishment of coalition politics in Northern Ireland is seen as being a precarious task.

Assess the success or otherwise of the non-sectarian political parties in Northern Ireland.

Examine why key political figures, such as Gerry Adams and the Reverend Ian Paisley, play such a significant role in Northern Irish politics.

Helpful websites

www.allianceparty.org Alliance Party

www.dup.org.uk Democratic Unionist Party

www.niwc.org.uk Northern Ireland Women's Coalition

www.pup-ni.org.uk Progressive Unionist Party

www.sdlp.ie SDLP

www.sinnfein.ie Sinn Fein

www.uup.org Ulster Unionist Party

www.cain.ulst.ac.uk for more information on political parties in Northern Ireland.

Suggestions for further reading

J. Coakley (ed.), *Changing Shades of Orange and Green*, University College Dublin Press, 2002.

B. Feeney, *Sinn Fein: A Hundred Turbulent Years*, O'Brien Press, 2002.

J. Tonge, *The New Northern Irish Politics?*, Palgrave, 2005.

CHAPTER 12

Creeping Federalism or a Unitary State?

Contents

Overview

This final chapter seeks to answer the question posed by its title: 'Creeping federalism or a unitary state?' It starts by examing the extent of the changes made by devolution to the way we are governed. The chapter then defines federalism, its component parts, and those that desire it and oppose it within the United Kingdom. It asks and answers the question, 'does devolution mean the same as federalism?' We have seen in the previous chapters how politicians have stated that the process of political devolution is evolving all the time. It is likely, however, that each part of the United Kingdom will develop separately from every other. This is what is described as 'a rolling programme' which best fits the political realities of local circumstances. London, Scotland, Wales and Northern Ireland have started the process. Over time, the English regions may or may not follow suit. Since devolution has been introduced, it has been stated by many political commentators that Britain has become 'quasi-federal' or that 'creeping federalism is the order of the day'. Often these accusations are made on the simple assumption that devolution is the same as federalism. This final chapter examines the evidence that Britain is now, or will shortly become, a federal state.

Key issues to be covered in this chapter

- What devolution has achieved
- What is meant by federalism
- Is Britain now a federal state?
- Independence as an alternative to devolution and federalism

What has devolution achieved?

In January 2005, after examining the development and processes of devolution in Britain for much of the previous decade the Economic and Social Research Council's (ESRC) Research Programme on Devolution and Constitutional Change was able to conclude with six key points that can be stated about devolution in Britain:

1. Relations between central and devolved government reveal minimal change from the pre-devolution arrangement for dealing with Scottish, Welsh and Northern Irish matters, relying on bilateral and informal links largely among officials and not ministers.

2. There are few meetings between British and devolved administrators, and there are special arrangements in some policy fields such as agriculture and European Union matters.

3. The Treasury retains considerable powers over devolved finance though it lacks levers, such as public-service agreements, which it can use on Whitehall departments.

4. The apparatus at the centre for dealing with devolution is small and has a limited brief, and Whitehall departments have done little to differentiate between their England-only, England-and-Wales, and British functions.

5. Neither Westminster nor Whitehall has sought to adapt the legislative process to create different categories of legislation according to which territories and functions they affect.

6. The pattern of minimal alteration has made a major constitutional change a straightforward administrative and legal process, but one vulnerable to disputes created by future changes of government.

Despite the fact that devolution has not radically altered the government at Westminster, one of the major fears expressed by the Conservatives and by other opponents of devolution was that Britain would be seperated into a series of states or that a 'creeping federalism' would occur in which Westminster and the government in London would become increasingly irrelevant. In the past the opponents of devolution were often the opponents of '**federalism**' too. But, as we shall see, the two are very different.

What exactly is federalism?

With the advent of political devolution in the United Kingdom, the question can be asked 'Is Britain becoming a federal state?' Interest in federalism as a political concept has been awakened.

Originally the term 'federalism' described 'a loose alliance or union of states for limited purposes, usually military or commercial'. Today, we would describe such an alliance as a 'confederacy'. In the eighteenth century, however, the United States came into existence. This created a form of government in which the central government and the governments of the various states had considerable powers but, at the same time, they had **independence** from one another. The key components of federalism are shown in Box 12.1. Federalism has some distinct advantages.

- *It distributes power between the central body and peripheral ones.* In its entirely, power is held neither centrally or locally, but distributed between the two. The **sovereignty** of the state is divided among two or more levels, with each one being supreme in its own defined area.
- *It gives regional and local interests constitutionally guaranteed political voices,* within the region and nationally. Central government cannot ignore the wishes and desires of other areas.
- *It creates a 'network of checks and balances'* to help counteract an ambitious central government. Central government cannot have its wish on every matter unless it has the agreement of the federal states.
- *Federalism helps unite fragmented and differing societies into one united political mechanism.* Some countries are so large or so diverse in their ethnic mixes that a unitary system would make government very difficult and remote.

Federalism also has a number of drawbacks. The major ones are:

- *Over the last century, there has been a tendency towards greater centralisation of government throughout the world.* This has meant that federalism has become less important. Even within the federal state, much of the power and the tax-raising ability are in the hands of central (federal), rather than state, government.

- *Federal states can often be weak and divided by the different societies within them.* This can lead to less effective government overall.
- *By constraining the central government, decision-making can be slow or is often timid.* Bold policies, which are sometimes needed in times of economic hardship, are harder to get through central government.
- *It can be difficult to get all of the federal states to agree on important issues* because of vested interest within each. Many of the federal states will compete with one another for inward investment projects with no clear arbitrator to decide to whom it should go.
- *There are continual power battles over where sovereignty lies.* Even in systems where the constitution appears to define the exact powers of each level, there are continual battles over who has supreme sovereignty concerning certain issues.
- *It may not decrease the desire for independence from some of its constituant members.* This is perhaps most notable in Canada where the francophone province of Quebec has held a number of referendums on independence.

Box 12.1 The components of federalism

There are certain features that are common to most federal systems:

Two relatively autonomous levels of government. Both central (federal) and regional (state) governments possess a range of powers which the other cannot encroach upon.

Written constitution. The responsibilities and powers of each level of government are defined in a written or codified constitution.

Constitutional arbitrator. Any disputes between state and federal government can be settled by a supreme court.

Linking institutions. To foster co-operation and understanding between federal and state-level governments each region is given a voice in the central policy-making. This is achieved through a bicameral legislature (two chambers) in which the states normally have representation in the second, or upper, chamber.

The background to desiring federalism in Britain

Although the Westminster parliament has helped establish federal systems around the world, in countries such as Australia, Canada and Germany, it has never felt the desire to repeat the experiment in the United Kingdom. On the few occasions federalism has been considered seriously by governments or by Royal Commissions, it has been dismissed. The 1973 Royal (Kilbrandon) Commission on the Constitution, for instance, dismissed federalism as a viable model. Before, and since, the Kilbrandon Commission, the Liberal Democrat Party has been the most pro-federalist political party in Britain. Liberal Democrat policies have continually advocated implementing some of the measures in Box 12.1, such as turning the House of Lords into 'an elected second chamber capable of representing the nations and regions of the UK'.

The Labour Party has often been torn between those members who want devolution and those who prefer a unitary system of government. There are few within the party who have advocated a federal Britain. Currently, the official Labour Party line is that devolution in Wales and Scotland has run its course and that, in England, it will develop only on a regional basis.

In the twentieth century, however, the dominant political party in Britain has been the Conservative Party. As we saw in the earlier chapters, it has always been a strongly unionist party which wishes to see a unitary system of government based at Westminster. This certainly rules out a federal Britain.

Does devolution mean the same as federalism?

Since devolution has been introduced in Britain, there has been much confusion over whether or not Britain has become a federal state. This is not the case, although this might occur in the future. In its present form, devolution establishes a far greater measure of decentralisation in Britain's unitary system of government than has occurred since the Middle Ages. It stops short, however, of the transition into a federal system.

Devolution therefore differs from federalism in that, though the political units may cover the same territorial areas, devolved bodies share no sovereignty with central government. Their responsibilities and powers are derived from, and are conferred, the centre (Westminster). Box 12.1 shows us the component parts of federalism. None of these is apparent in the United Kingdom at present.

Instead of written constitutional relationships between the assemblies, Scottish Parliament and the government in Whitehall are ruled by a series of departmental 'concordats'. These relationships are not specified in a written constitution, as would be the case in a federal structure. The concordats are agreements between the devolved institutions and Whitehall departments concerning their respective roles and responsibilities. They set the ground rules for 'administrative co-operation and exchange of information'.

The Scotland Act (1998) created a Scottish Parliament with legislative powers over all matters not expressly 'reserved' to the British Parliament. Reserved matters include such issues as foreign and defence policy, the management of the British macro-economic system, European Union issues, and social security. Most importantly, Section 28 (7) of the 1998 act states that having a Scottish Parliament 'does not affect the power of the Parliament of the United Kingdom to make laws for Scotland'. In addition to this, in the *Memorandum of Understanding*, that sets out the underlying principles between the Westminster government and the devolved institutions, the first two paragraphs state:

> The United Kingdom Parliament retains authority on any issue, whether devolved or not.

> The United Kingdom Parliament retains the absolute right to debate, enquire into or make representations about devolved matters.

In principle, therefore because it retains ultimate sovereignty, the Westminster parliament can overturn any law made by the Scottish Parliament or secondary legislation brought about by the Welsh Assembly. In Wales, the Westminster parliament continues to be the principal law-maker. Therefore, the assembly can only shape legislation around the edges or negotiate with Westminster to have specific legislation created for it. In a federal structure, state and federal governments are able to make laws which can be 'struck down' only by the body that made them or by the Supreme Court because that law is unconstitutional (contrary to the articles of the written constitution).

Indications that Britain is not turning into a federal state

There is a number of indicators that make it quite clear that British government policy is not leading Britain into a federal state. Although the New Labour government has carried out a wealth of constitutional change, it has not sought to go down the route of federalism. This is clear from a number of decisions made by the Labour government:

- *A federal Britain would result in the transfer of sovereignty from Westminster to the devolved governments.* Westminster has retained ultimate sovereignty on all issues relating to the devolved bodies although, *in reality, it cedes these to them on many issues of domestic policy.*

- *A federal Britain would require a written constitution.* There has been no attempt to write a codified constitution which states the role, function and power of the new devolved institutions and enshrine them in law. This would be a necessary step for a federal Britain to evolve. Although the Human Rights Act 2000 is sometimes cited as the nearest Britain has to a constitution, it does not define the mechanisms by which Britain should be governed.

- *The devolved forms of government would need to have a direct voice in central government.* This will not occur. In its report of January 2000, the Royal Commission on the Reform of the House of Lords stated that there should be a regional element in any future House of Lords. It did not say, however, that these members should come directly from the devolved institutions. Similarly, further attempts at reforming the House of Lords have not mentioned any representation from the devolved institutions.

- *The devolved institutions would need greater fiscal independence.* This would prevent the Westminster government from determining its policies by 'holding the purse strings of finance'. The majority of taxation in the United Kingdom is undertaken by central government. The Scottish Parliament has tax-raising powers but does not use them. The other devolved bodies do not have tax-raising powers and there are currently no plans to give them any. In federal systems, such as those of the United States and Switzerland, this figure is about 15 per cent.

- *The devolved institutions would need to have their own civil services.* It is said that 'no man can serve two masters' because he/she will have divided loyalties. In this case, loyalties would be divided between the state and the federal government. The devolved bodies have their own administrative staffs which are independent of the Civil service. Northern Ireland also has its own separate civil service. On the whole, however, those civil servants serving the Welsh and Scottish governments are still members of the British Civil Service.

- *The devolved bodies should be able to determine their own policy with as little interference from Westminster and Whitehall as possible.* The Westminster government continues to determine policy in the devolved bodies despite resistance from those bodies. Performance-related pay for teachers was introduced in Wales even though the assembly voted against the measure. Similarly, the boxer Mike Tyson was allowed into Scotland despite the fact that the Scottish Parliament was opposed to it.

Box 12.2 Independence an alternative to devolution or federalism

Plaid Cymru and the Scottish National Party believe that Wales and Scotland should become independent countries within the European Union. Plaid Cymru's aim is 'to secure self-government for Wales and a democratic Welsh state, based on socialist principles . . . To secure for Wales the right to become a member of the United Nations Organisation.' Whereas, the Scottish National Party 'aims to create a just, caring and enterprising society in the mainstream of modern Europe by realising Scotland's full potential as an independent nation.' Plaid Cymru and the SNP have noted how successful Ireland has been since joining the European Economic Community in 1974 and the extent to which it has been able to transform its economy with the use of European Union structural funds.

Plaid Cymru is particularly keen on the concept of a federal Europe in which Europe takes over some of the key strategic roles, such as general taxation, and major economic and foreign-policy issues. Under this, Wales would have 'self-determination' or, in essence, it would become a federal state within a 'federal Europe'. Such a notion would allow an easier route to independence by cushioning the costs associated with breaking away.

- *The devolved state parliaments would all need to have primary law-making powers.* Currently only Northern Ireland and the Scottish Parliament have primary legislative powers. There are no plans to give these to London, and Wales has a mechanism for getting its own bills through the Houses of Parliament but it cannot create them in Cardiff.
- *A truly federal Britain would involve parliaments for the English regions as well.* Although new regional development agencies have been established in England outside London, attempts to turn these into elected regional chambers have failed. Therefore, with the exception of London, devolution in the United Kingdom, holds only for the Celtic countries. The prospect of having a law-making parliament for England similar to that in Scotland was permanently ruled out by the Labour Government early in 2006.

Conclusion

We have seen that devolution is very different from federalism. It is clear from government policy that Britain is far from being, or even becoming, a federal country. Central government still remains the overwhelming dominant political power in Britain, and political sovereignty remains in Westminster. The policies of the Conservatives and the Labour Party will not lead to a federal Britain. Although the Liberal Democrats do desire a federal Britain, they are not strong enough, politically, to achieve this. The nationalist parties desire straight independence, or union with Ireland in the case of Northern Ireland, rather than federalism.

At the same time as federalism is being dismissed within Britain, the role of Europe is growing in determining policy issues not only at a Westminster but also at a sub-Westminster level in Wales. Policy issues, such as agriculture, are often determined directly by the European Union with little direct involvement from the devolved institution within Britain. Here, Westminster has ceded sovereignty to the European Union and, therefore, the devolved institutions must also take account other European issues such as the European Convention on Human Rights in their executive duties, and law- and policy-making. It may be the case, therefore, that there is a federal Europe well before there is a federal Britain.

. . . .

What you should have learnt from reading this chapter

- While devolution has reshaped the way that the Celtic nations are governed, it has made little impact on the government at Westminster.

- It has been asserted that Britain has become a federal state but there is no evidence to support this view.

- Independence for Scotland and for Wales is still viewed as an alternative to devolution or federalism by some nationalist political parties.

Glossary of key terms

Federalism A form of government in which both the central government and sub-central (national or regional) governments enjoy considerable power but remain independent from one another and are linked together as one 'country'.

Independence The removal of a region or the division of a nation so that the control of that area is held solely within its borders and is no longer held by the nation/region to which it was previously joined.

Sovereignty The supreme power of the political institution with respect to its legitimate legal authority.

Likely examination questions

Comment on the view that devolution has had no real impact on the way that Britain is run.

To what extent is it true to say that, through devolution, the United Kingdom has turned into a federal state?

Helpful websites

http://www.ucl.ac.uk/constitution-unit/ University College, London's Constitution Unit's devolution programme which provides information on how devolution has developed in the United Kingdom.

http://www.federalunion.org.uk The Federal Union has a website which details how a federal structure of government would work in the United Kingdom.

http://www.devolution.ac.uk/ The Economic and Social Research Council ran a large-scale research project from 2000 to 2005 on the 'Devolution and Constitutional Change Programme' which covers much of devolutionary development, including aspects of federalism.

Suggestions for further reading

V. Bogdanor, *Devolution in the United Kingdom*, Opus, 1999.

R. Deacon, *Devolution in Britain Today*, Manchester University Press, 2006

P. Dunleavy, A. Gamble, R. Heffernan and G. Peele, *Developments in British Politics*, Palgrave, 2004.

B. Markesinis and J. Fedtke (eds), *Patterns of Regionalism and Federalism: Lessons for the UK*, Vol. 8 (Clifford Chance Lectures), Hart Publishing, 2006.

W. Norman and D. Karmis (eds), *Theories of Federalism: A Reader*, Palgrave, 2005.

Index

Bold indicates that the term is defined